The Message

THE INCREDIBLE TRUE STORY OF THE KNOCK VISIONARY

JOE COLEMAN

POOLBEG

Published 2010
by Poolbeg Books Ltd.
123 Grange Hill, Baldoyle,
Dublin 13, Ireland
Email: poolbeg@poolbeg.com

1 3 5 7 9 10 8 6 4 2

A catalogue record for this book is available from the British Library.

ISBN 978-1-84223-443-3

Typeset by Patricia Hope in Sabon

Printed by
CPI Cox & Wyman, UK

www.poolbeg.com

This book is a tribute to my fellow visionary
the late Keith Henderson

Contents

For what does it profit a man to gain the whole world, and forfeit his soul?

MARK 8:36

Foreword

Why a Book on Miracles and Apparitions in the Twenty-first Century?

When is the last time you thought about life after death? Not the most positive of subjects, but admit it: it's something that is always at the back of your mind. Yet it's not a subject you tend to speak openly about to your family or friends. Privately, though, you ask the same questions, over and over again. What actually happens after death? Does God really exist? Is there really such a place as Heaven or Hell?

Most of us want to believe in a spiritual world. We really do. This world is too harsh for most people to face alone. True believers have the enviable luxury and comfort of believing in a God and the afterlife. For others, however, a lack of belief in God or a spiritual world means they tend not to think about death; they block the subject out and simply live life for today. Let's face it, it's extremely difficult to believe in something you can't see, feel or hear.

It is especially difficult to keep faith alive in a modern and materialistic world. A world where, at a flick of a button, we can access any kind of stimulant or entertainment to suit all tastes. What chance, therefore, does a visit to your local church compare with the latest episode of *X-Factor*, *Spooks* or *Oprah*?

However, very few people would argue against the fact that every aspect of life as we once knew it seems to be caught in a never-ending struggle, fraught with negative connotations. Very few countries in the world today have been left unscathed by severe economic downturn, political corruption, greed, crime, climate change and natural disasters. Whichever way you look at it, one thing is clear: the world as we know it is experiencing a type of upheaval.

It is said that any such crisis prompts people to examine their lives and their spirituality and results in an urge to "get back to basics". Some will argue that vulnerable people at times of strife will grasp at anything that smacks of a positive outcome. That is the sceptics' argument, but it can equally be argued that such crises strip away the material things of life and force us to acknowledge deeper truths.

Whatever the motivation, if you look back over the past decade, more people than ever are publicly declaring their belief in a spiritual world. This is particularly evident in the United States. According to a national poll published in the United States in 2008, 92% of Americans believe in God or a "universal spirit" – including one in five of those who call themselves atheists. More than half of Americans said they prayed at least once a day. While 81% claim to believe in Heaven, 70% believe in Satan and 69% believe in Hell. Over 80% of Americans, according to international research group Gallup, believe in angels. A *Washington Post* survey in 2008 showed that the majority of Americans believe in a "higher power" guiding them in the world, with nearly 80% claiming they think that miracles do occur. It also found that over half of Americans pray at least once a day. In Europe, where Christianity is in freefall, the picture is quite different. According to a Eurobarometer Poll in 2005 certain countries showed a significant drop in the number of people who claim to believe in a God. In the UK, for example, according to the survey only 38% of the population believes in God. Europe tends to be segmented and no two countries are alike when it comes to belief in God. For example, in Sweden only about 23% believe in God while in countries such as Spain more than 59% believe and in Italy the figure jumps to 74%. In Ireland it shows that 73% believe in God (a drop from 94% in a poll in 1999). In a separate question, when asked "Does religion occupy an important part of your life?" 75% of people in France said it didn't, as did 71% in the UK, 59% in Spain and 42% in Ireland.

Yet, against this background there has been a strange surge in belief in angels and the Devil! 38% of Britons, for example, claim to believe in angels while 29% believe in the Devil. This compares to 80% in the US who believe in angels and 70% who believe in the Devil.

A belief, too, in Marian apparitions is on the increase. Tens of millions of people from around the world are conducting pilgrimages and creating prayer groups as a direct result of the Marian apparition phenomena. An estimated one million pilgrims, for example, of all ages and from all over the world, visit Medjugorje each year. This is despite the fact that Medjugorje has not yet been officially recognised by the Vatican (although in March 2010 the Pope finally announced the setting up of a commission to investigate it – almost thirty years after the first apparition was reported).

Over 386 cases of Marian apparitions were reported from 1900 to 1966 and presented to the Holy See of Rome for investigation. Only eight were fully approved; eleven were deemed "neutral" (this means that they are being viewed with an open mind), sixty-eight were deemed negative and 299 are still under investigation. The eight that were approved are Fatima, Portugal; Beauraing and Banneux, Belgium; Akita, Japan; Syracuse, Italy; Zeitun, Egypt; Manila, Philippines; and Betania, Venezuela. In all of these cases, it is claimed that Our Lady delivered some very specific messages, usually requesting people to pray for repentance; some are frightening and are a warning to the Church and people all over the world to change their ways.

So as atheism seems to be on the rise in Europe, why is it that belief in angels, Marian apparitions, the Devil and the supernatural is on the increase? Could it be to do with a search for a new spiritual focus? Are people waking up to the fact that materialism no longer has the power to fulfil us?

When people are infected with corruption and human greed, the wealth and worldly goods they possess will eventually collapse. That is a trend you can see replicated time and time again throughout history. It could be argued that unnatural levels of economic wealth and greed are responsible for the mess we find ourselves in today. Over the last decade, an economic boom elevated many people in the western world to a lifestyle that they would not have believed possible before. Many working-class people noticed little difference, but for the middle and higher income brackets, their personal assets snowballed to extraordinary levels. Many people, especially in Ireland, got carried away and borrowed excessively to build assets. Then – wham! It all came tumbling down. It happened so quickly it took their breath away. It left in its wake a sour taste of bitterness, disappointment, fear, guilt, and, perhaps more than anything, a feeling of utter despair, bewilder-ment and hopelessness.

Even in such a context, for those who evaluate their worth on their material success, it is very difficult to believe in a spiritual supernatural world. How can the materialistic people of the modern-day world be expected to believe in a miracle – something they cannot see, hear, touch or smell – or which they have not personally witnessed?

A Visionary who Speaks with Our Lady

What if someone could prove to you that God really does exist? That there is an afterlife – a different state of being, where you will get to meet your loved ones again? You would probably jump up and down for joy initially. Imagine, then, how it would be when the message sinks in, how you would feel incredible happiness and peace – peace that you never thought you would experience in this lifetime. Because you would finally know for sure that life does not end here. Our life on this Earth is simply a passage in time.

This book is about one such man who claims that the apparitions and visions he sees of Our Lady at the Holy Shrine of Knock in County Mayo, Ireland, and the messages that she brings to the world, will change the way we think about things forever. His name is Joe Coleman and he describes himself as a visionary of Our Lady and a "seer".

Joe Coleman was born in the Marian Year of 1954,

the first in Church history: the year when Catholics were asked to focus on Mary by Pope Pius XII. During this year hundreds of grottos devoted to Our Lady were created throughout Ireland. Joe was born in the month of May, the month traditionally devoted to Mary.

Joe is a simple, working-class man of little education who comes from Ballyfermot, Dublin. Known as a kind and holy man, Joe was born with special gifts, which he claims include healing powers both of a physical and spiritual nature. Joe claims to possess psychic ability: he says he has been able to see "spirit people" regularly since he was a young child. Many of these spirits are strangers, according to him, who ask him to pass on messages to their loved ones. Others are simply lost and cannot pass into the next life. He helps them, through what he calls "spiritual rescue".

Joe never courted any kind of public attention during his years as a healer and seer, yet he suddenly found himself in the middle of one of the most frenzied media events in Ireland when he first drew attention to the fact that he had begun to receive messages from Our Lady from April 2009 onward. He found himself the target of hate, outrage and controversy. Despite the fact that many people have backed him up and have posted images and videos and commented online about their views and experiences, he was laughed at, scorned, ridiculed and made the subject of abusive verbal attack.

Joe believes that the apparitions that have taken place

in Knock during 2009 and 2010 are miracles and that they prove that God exists. Moreover, he claims that God is trying to communicate with the world through Our Lady, the Virgin Mary, who has been sent by God and who does not come of her own accord.

All of the apparitions, Joe says, were promised by Our Lady in advance. She gave him exact times and dates, which he made public. Thousands of other people claim to have witnessed not one but a series of apparitions of the Virgin Mary at the Holy Shrine in Knock during 2009 and 2010. A dancing sun, images of crosses in the sky, images of Our Lady, of Padre Pio and of Our Lord are just some of the visions claimed to have been seen by many. All of these apparitions happened at the same predicted time – immediately after the 3.00 p.m. Rosary was said – on the predicted dates. They were reported all over the world in the media, on the internet and by those who witnessed the events.

Joe claims to have received many messages from Our Lady. Some have been made public and given to the media but very few of these have been published. Other secret messages, he says, cannot be revealed until a much later time. The messages have been given by Our Lady to awaken our spiritual minds, to open our hearts to believing in God again, and to protect His children from the illusions and temptations provided by Satan. All the messages, Joe claims, relate specifically to a world in serious spiritual crisis, at a time of great global suffering, and their aim is to inform the world that we must pray to restore our spirituality. Joe believes that the messages are being imparted and are significant in that they relate to a time of great change in the world.

For some, especially those who were at the actual events, the apparitions have brought tremendous joy. It has converted others back to their belief in God, irrespective of what religion they follow – if any. For Joe Coleman and those who believe what he says, it has brought spiritual peace back into their lives. As he says, the greatest illness in society today is a sickness of the soul, not of the body.

For the sceptics, particularly those who did not attend the events, it has caused anger and outrage. "How dare these people make such claims?" "What gives them the right to deliberately mislead people in a scam, a deliberate attempt to deceive?" As for the Catholic Church, in some quarters news of the apparitions has been received with great joy – in other sectors it is claimed that it has caused deep offence and they condemn the apparitions.

Support for Joe Coleman is, despite everything, still very strong not only in Ireland but around the world. People from the US, the UK, Israel, Brazil, India and China attended the apparitions and support him through letters and email. They claim to have seen the sun dance as well as other images in the sky during the apparitions and have been following events with intense interest.

In the middle of the scramble to "expose" Joe as a "fraud", very few people have paid any heed to the actual messages. With the exception of one newspaper which published the first two messages he received, none of the other media published them despite the fact that they were given them. So the public are not actually aware of the content of the messages.

The sceptics think Joe Coleman is either mad, deluded or a downright fraud. The cynics think he's looking for media attention. As for those who believe him, you have to ask yourself why do they believe? What did they see that convinced them?

Joe says he never set out to "become a visionary", no more than any of the other visionaries who have claimed to have received messages from Our Lady. More than happy to enjoy the privilege of receiving such messages privately, Joe says that they now have to be made public due to their serious nature. Because these messages, according to Joe, have a direct relationship to the Second Coming of Jesus Christ on Earth. According to the messages, which are contained in this book, the world will begin to change beyond recognition very soon. It has been revealed to him by the Virgin Mary that Christ will walk the Earth again. And that time is very near.

Margaret E Moore

Preface

I did not set out to write a book. When I was asked to consider documenting the full story of the apparitions in Knock, County Mayo, and elsewhere, my first reaction was a firm "no". I was unsure of public reaction and, to be brutally honest, I was scared. I had just come out the other side of a media frenzy which I had found very difficult to handle.

Since the apparitions of our Blessed Mother, the Virgin Mary, Mother of God, began in 2007, my life has changed beyond recognition. While I had been blessed with spiritual gifts from a very young age, nothing could have prepared me for the role into which I have been propelled to assume responsibility for communicating the messages given to me by Our Blessed Mother, the Virgin Mother of God.

I have been overwhelmed by the experience and moved to a state of complete belief in God which is extremely difficult to describe. While I always possessed a firm belief in God, Jesus Christ and Our Blessed Mother, I could not describe myself, before the apparitions, as an exceptionally "holy person". No – like all of us, I consider myself a sinner. I have been called a "Holy Joe" by the media but this is far from the truth. Yes, I have always had a spiritual gift, in that I believe I am psychic and have been blessed with healing powers. However, it is only since I began seeing Our Blessed Mother and receiving her messages that I truly believe.

The best way to describe how I feel as a result is a mix of profound shock, humility, joy, confusion, love, wonder and excitement. Excitement – because I have received absolute proof of what I had half-believed all those years: that there is a Heaven and a Hell. It's that simple. Despite the varied content of the messages I have received from Our Blessed Mother, they all point to one thing. There is a God, there is a Heaven, there is a purgatory and a Hell. Then there is "The Deceiver", otherwise known as Satan. Yes, he exists. But he is so cunning that most people will simply smile and say, "Oh yeah, really?" I hope to show, in this book, based on the messages received by Our Lady, how he operates and how he has set out to destroy us by turning all of us away from believing in a spiritual world.

I found it difficult to accept that Our Lady chose me as her messenger. After all, who am I? A middle-aged, uneducated, working-class man, unemployed for years due to a serious accident. This was the part I found hard to accept. Why me, in the name of God? But accept it I did. Because I eventually realised that these events have a profound meaning for all of us.

Some of the public reaction has been extremely negative. In fairness, much of that was down to the way I handled some interviews – I was not prepared and was very inexperienced. I could not even face the media for a period of time from December 2009 up to February 2010.

The last thing I expected when I went public about the apparitions and the visions I was receiving was the public backlash against me. My intentions were good. In all honesty, I found it all very tough. Yet it was necessary.

I now feel it is my duty to set out clearly the essential facts about the messages received from Our Lady so far. I have to let everyone know what challenges lie ahead of us in the coming years as the full meaning of the Book of Revelations becomes more apparent. The world is changing. The Second Coming *will* happen. I have an obligation to tell this story – a story which is really not mine at all.

Only two of these messages have been published before. None of the others have up to now. Everyone in the world has a right to know what they contain, because the messages concern all of us everywhere. These messages, at the beginning, were simple and loving in nature. They have, however, taken on a more urgent tone and I would beg anyone reading this book to keep a completely open mind before you judge.

Most people view those who claim to see spirits, or who have experienced inexplicable psychic events, as having overactive imaginations. They judge them harshly. They view people like me as being on a fool's quest for popularity. We're seen as superstitious, hysterical – living in a make-believe world. Even worse, we are often viewed as being deliberately deceitful, preying on people's vulnerability. Other non-believers simply view the whole thing as pure and utter nonsense – not even worth discussion. How wrong they all are.

It is only when you experience face-to-face confrontation with Satan, the Evil One, that any doubts you may have had in the past about the spirit world evaporate instantly.

There are just too many reported occurrences for belief in the phenomenon to be fobbed off by scientists or atheists. The challenge for the sceptics becomes even more difficult when they try to disprove the increasing number of reported spiritual signals around the world, such as apparitions of Our Blessed Mother, Our Lady, as well as those reported within religions other than Christianity. For my part, I know that God does not favour one religion over another. Because he loves all his children equally, he wants all of us to understand divine manifestations. It is one of his ways to prove his existence. But it is only one way.

As more people continue publicly to claim spiritual

sightings, experiences, events and visions, you have to ask yourself why these are happening. Look at the well-documented and renowned apparition of Our Lady at Fatima in Portugal, where 70,000 people publicly claimed to have witnessed a miracle. How can you argue with that? The scientists still didn't believe, despite the fact that the time and place of this event was predicted in advance.

How do you explain those people cured from a terminal illness through prayer, or a visit to, say, Lourdes? Even when these cures can be backed up medically, the sceptics still won't believe. There really is no satisfactory answer, because none of the normal rules apply to the spirit world.

I would like to thank Margaret E Moore, my ever-patient co-writer who has been working tirelessly with me to produce this book. I would also like to thank all those wonderful loving people, those with deep faith in God, who have believed in my authenticity right from the start. And also those non-believers who came to Knock as total sceptics and who were converted by the proof they saw with their own eyes. Now, they and the rest of those who went to Knock during the recent apparitions, know for a fact that not only does God exist but he is trying to communicate with us urgently, through his messenger Our Blessed Mother, the Virgin Mary, Queen of Heaven.

Joseph Coleman, March 2010

Beginnings

1

A Spiritual Encounter

I saw my first apparition of the Blessed Virgin Mary at the age of twelve. It happened in a little room in my grandmother's house, in the heart of Dublin on Pearse Street, at three o'clock in the afternoon.

My grandmother had gone to the post office to collect her pension and I was left alone. I remember idly looking around the room and glancing at the double bed in the corner. I noticed a picture of Our Lady, which I hadn't seen before, on the wall over the iron bed. As I stared at the image, the room seemed to become very still, very quiet.

In a scene of utter silence, while the world seemed to come to a grinding halt, I noticed that a strange type of mist began to waft slowly from the picture towards me. Blinking in surprise, I focused on the picture again. *God, it's still there*, I thought. It was definitely a mist of some sort. I felt a sudden and inexplicable urge to kneel down and pray. I gazed nervously upwards, my face fixed on the image of Our Lady. She seemed to float from the picture and emerge slowly, but surely, from the frame. I was frozen, rooted to the spot, as her image grew bigger and bigger until she seemed to float towards me in what I can only describe as a hazy cloud of blues and pinks.

Then she beamed at me, with the most beautiful, radiant and haunting smile imaginable, a smile bursting with such utter love and tenderness that it filled me with a powerful, overwhelming sense of joy. I had never experienced such feelings before and they permeated every ounce of my being. Then it was over just as quickly as it had begun.

My head spinning with confusion and shock, I stumbled out of the room and somehow managed to run as fast as my legs could carry me straight out the hall door. Terrified now and unsure of what I had just seen, I ran all the way down Pearse Street and never looked back. I kept what I saw a secret for a long time and it was only in later years that I told my mother.

Childhood Spirit Friends

From my youngest days, I can remember seeing "events" and "people" which in fact other people couldn't, though I didn't realise that at the time. I assumed that everyone else could see what I saw. I made comments to my mother which now I realise would have been perceived as being "odd". I saw people she didn't see. I spoke with them. They spoke with me. My mother at first thought that they were my "imaginary friends" and that I was just an imaginative child.

As I had been seeing spirits since I was a young child, I couldn't tell the difference between the spirits of dead people and people in the flesh. They looked exactly the same to me. It was only when they disappeared that I would know they were "spirit people". They were simply there one minute and gone the next.

My mother made allowances for me. Quieter than other children, I was considered a little shy by some, withdrawn by others, and to those who did not know me I was considered antisocial. I always preferred my own company to mixing with other children. For example, I always liked to play in the back garden on my own, while my brothers and sisters palled around with their friends on the main road outside our house. I didn't mind. I always had children to play with – but I was the only one who saw them. I called them my "spirit friends".

My mother was blessed with a great Dublin sense of humour. When she would see me in the back garden, chatting away on my own, she would poke her head out the kitchen window and shout, "Joe, who are ya talking to today? Any new friends? What's their names?" Because each and every one of these "spirit children" had names, I would tell her. And when I dashed into the house, excited and bursting with my news, she would touch my face gently, cup it in her hands and give me a tight hug. I would then be given a job to do and all would be forgotten.

My mother was a very humble person and a very loving woman. While she would be very patient with me, she warned me to keep my secrets to myself. "Joe, that's a great story – but don't be telling everyone that." She would dismiss me with a loving but firm wave of her hand. But from the time I was seven years old, she began to react differently to my stories, taking me more seriously.

I began to tell my mother details about the messages these little friends of mine would reveal. Some of these messages would relate directly to people she knew personally, my parents' friends and neighbours. What disturbed my mother most was the fact that I revealed them in advance. How she laughed at first! She'd scold me, saying, "Joe, you have an overactive mind, so you have! You are a right little character, aren't you?" And she'd laugh. But that was only in the beginning.

One day I told my mother I had dreamed about a neighbour of ours the previous night. I told her I saw him walking through the back garden in a brown habit – the common habit used in funeral homes at the time. It was only when this same neighbour died the following day that she began to take my predictions seriously.

She began to believe that I had a gift of some sort. After that, there were many occasions when stories or events happened exactly as I had predicted. That's when she became worried, scared and overly protective of me.

My mother used to call me "a watcher". She'd say, "Look at Joe, he never misses a trick." I watched what was going on. I took everything in, and it was nothing to do with curiosity. It's not just that I was aware of what was going on around me; I would also sense things, things that sometimes made me very uncomfortable. For example, I was always quick to sense an atmosphere in a room. I knew instinctively when I was in a negative atmosphere, where people would start a row, even before it began. I noticed people's moods instantly, irrespective of the look they had on their faces. For example if they were ill I could spot the illness and the source of it straight away. I would know if it related to their throat, their bowels, their heart, their kidneys, their head or some other part of their body and I could tell, immediately, if they were in recovery or if their condition was getting worse. There were times, of course, when I would keep my mouth shut, especially if I saw a black aura of some kind around them. Because I could sense imminent death, possibly days, weeks or even months before a person would die, I knew instinctively that it would have been wrong of me to reveal this kind of information. That was hard. And I would get upset when I knew that people were going to die soon.

Growing up in Ballyfermot, a very poor neighbourhood, during the late 1950s and early 1960s was difficult. Even if you were used to having nothing, it was still a tough place to live. Unemployment crippled our community. Putting basic food on the table was a daily struggle. Getting new clothes was considered a luxury and eating meat more than once a week was a treat. Many children were without proper shoes.

Ballyfermot was different to other Dublin suburbs. You see, it was built from scratch to rehouse families who had been uprooted from the tenement slums in Dublin city centre. This made-to-measure community offered little in the way of employment because there were no industrial facilities nearby. Yet the true spirit of Dublin city managed to stay alive. The Dublin sense of wit and humour managed to rise above the hardship and a real sense of community existed. People looked after each other then in Ballyer, as it was, and still is, affectionately known.

One thing about Ballyer which made it a far cry from life in the inner city was the fact there were fields nearby. We used to call them The Backers. To while away the time, and because I hated hanging around in groups of kids, I used to go up there. Some days I would find myself completely on my own there. I was drawn to an area of wild bushes, where I would see what I called "the little spirit people". They told me they were Earth angels. I would chat away with them and be mesmerised by some of the secrets they would tell me. It was completely fascinating and exciting. I was at my happiest then.

I was one of six surviving children. Our family had very little money. With only the bare necessities to survive on, we were no different from other families in the area. We had no TV in our house and everyone had to do their fair share of chores. I always helped out in the house and for some reason I was always given extra responsibility by my mother. Usually I was the one who was left to keep an eye on the other children at night if my parents had to go out, even though there were other siblings older than me. I was always obedient and did my best to please my parents. I was considered to be mature for my age. And while my parents recognised that I was different, a little "odd", I always had a deep sense of responsibility and they recognised that and always stood by me.

School in the 1960s

I was seven when I started school in St Louise's in Ballyfermot in 1961. I have no idea why I was sent to school so late, when most other kids started at the age of five. It was only later in life, when I was diagnosed as being dyslexic, that I wondered if my learning disability had something to do with it. Maybe my parents sent me to school at that late stage because they felt I wouldn't be able for it earlier. Either way, I was only in my new school a few weeks when I made my First Communion.

As a child I had a strong affinity with religion – probably an unusual thing for a child as young as seven. But I was always attracted to Our Lady of Lourdes for some reason. On the day I left the Junior School a few years later, they held a raffle. It was a penny for a ticket and the prize was a statue of Our Lady. I won it. I loved that statue. I felt safe with it under my arm and believed it would bring protection and light into my home. I don't know why I felt like this, but I had a secret love in my heart for this statue and for Our Lady. I kept the statue for a long time and then gave it as a present to my grandmother.

As I grew older my spiritual senses became stronger, and my attraction to people or animals who were sick became more pronounced. For example, if I saw a dog dying, I would see it leaving its body. Or if I saw a sick person, I would be drawn to that person, hoping to help them. I couldn't explain how I could "help them", but I wanted to touch them to make them better.

I understood that what I was experiencing was different to the norm but I couldn't give it a name. It felt perfectly normal to me and a natural part of me. But one thing was for sure. I realised that I had to be extremely careful what I said about these things to other people; otherwise they would look at me strangely or, worse, think I was deluded. So naturally

I was reluctant to talk openly about my experiences to anyone except for the few people I knew and trusted.

I found the secrecy frustrating, because I wanted to shout from the rooftops about what I was seeing. I wanted the world to know, but I couldn't say anything. I knew in my heart and soul that I stood out from other children. Despite my best efforts to be like the other kids, they still called me the "Goody Goody" or "Holy Joe". I was the focus of fun and amusement, but it was harmless bullying. And I didn't really care. I was also what they called a big softy – I was always doing favours for other kids. I was always the first to help out. Of course, kids such as me are always the first to be taken advantage of! Still, like all kids, I liked a bit of fun, joined in the local banter and got stuck into scuffles with other kids. I got used to being seen as the odd one out and in time it never bothered me or upset me. This was a good period in my life, but it was very short-lived.

After Junior School, I moved to Mary Queen of Angels School, also in Ballyfermot. I began to find school extremely difficult. I could not read or write properly. No matter how hard I tried I just couldn't master it. It was so upsetting. Little allowance was made by the teachers who, in hindsight, were not trained to be patient with the slower pupils during the 1960s. Remember, this was the time when physical punishment in schools was the norm; in schools the length and breadth of Ireland, the leather strap was used on the boys and the cane or the wooden ruler (known as the *bata*) was used on the girls. I remember the shame when I would be called to answer a question in front of the class. I would clam up and stand like an idiot while I'd be lambasted by a roaring master, his face contorted in a fierce red angry mass of pure fury.

Despite this, I had a great head for numbers and for learning the Catechism.

I liked the Catechism. It was the one subject that I didn't mind being asked about. I always felt Our Lady could get me through any tough questions I was asked. I really believed she helped me during that time. I knew the answer to every question and I knew all the Commandments off by heart.

I didn't really make any connection between Our Lady and the other spirits during this time. I didn't really see the spirits as being "religious" in any way, while Our Lady was someone we prayed to in school, the Mother of God and a very important part of our religion.

I finally managed to pass my Primary Certificate at the end of my time in primary school and got a pass in English, Irish, Maths and Religion. Because my grasp of reading and writing was still so poor I didn't go on to secondary school. This, of course, was fairly standard in those days, especially if your family had very little money. So I left school for good at thirteen years of age.

The Second Sight

I got my first job as a messenger for a mattress company on the corner of Lombard Street in Dublin's inner city. I stayed there for three or four weeks. I hated it. After that I trained to be a tailor. This was a fascinating job and I enjoyed the skills and got a kick out of seeing how a suit could be made from scratch.

It was during the lunch break one day that I noticed one of the staff sitting facing me. Suddenly, I blurted out to him unexpectedly, "My God, I can see bars around you – there's someone in prison belonging to you!" His jaw dropped and he stared long and hard at me. He asked me, "Where is he?" I told him he was in England. He nodded and told me that his son was, sadly, in prison. "How did you know? Did someone tell you – because I haven't told anyone." I told him about my gift.

After that I was constantly approached by other employees in the company, particularly during the breaks, when they would line up for a reading. I would sit at the table at lunch break. First I would hold the person's hand so that I could feel the energy field around them. It was then that I would be able to feel their thoughts and emotions and would, instantly, be able to tell them about various aspects of events, problems and other issues in their lives. I was nearly always spot on. Rarely did I get it wrong. Even I would be surprised by the accuracy of what I was able to reveal.

As word got around, kids in my neighbourhood

would ask me to tell their fortune. They'd be really excited and couldn't wait for me to do a "reading". I explained patiently time and time again that I was not a fortune-teller but someone who could see spirits and sense a lot about people's lives. Fortune-telling goes against everything God teaches us in terms of the dangers of "putting strange gods before Him". It didn't matter to them. They just saw me as someone who had a gift of some sort. But every time I did a reading there was a message behind it, and it was usually to give them some comfort in their lives. It was also, as I knew in the back of my mind, to try to ignite some kind of belief in the afterlife and the power of God. Yet all of this was a source of great amusement to these kids. I was a novelty. I enjoyed doing these readings. I felt I was bringing light into their world. To me it was the most natural thing in the world. I was in my element! I only wished, at the time, I could have earned a living doing this work.

Later in my teenage years I began to see spirits more clearly than ever before, spirits of people who had died. They would speak to me for a few minutes – usually to tell me they were happy in the new life. I was like a magnet and they kept coming to me. Sometimes it would get out of control and I would feel claustrophobic. *Why on earth are they talking to me?* I often asked myself. It was a constant source of amazement to me.

For instance, a Ballyfermot man whom I barely knew when he was alive began to appear to me to tell me he was okay in the spirit world. Puzzled, but not frightened, I just couldn't understand it. *Why me?* I said to myself. *I don't need to know!* Sometimes I found it extremely frustrating. *Why don't they leave me alone? Why did they feel the need to come to me, and what exactly do they want me to do?* It was even worse when I was going out with my friends, especially if I was heading off to a local disco!

It was also during this phase of my life that I became more attuned to one form of my spiritual gift. I would usually receive a message from spirits associated with various people – mostly relatives who had passed. This could happen in a local shop, at work, on the street or even on the bus. They would usually touch me and I'd feel a heat coming over me when they'd try to get my attention. They'd then give me a message for that person. I would deliver the message and the funny thing was that in most cases these people would listen and be astonished at the information I was giving them because it was so relevant to their lives. It's not something I would do every day obviously but only if I felt it was appropriate. In these cases too I would sometimes tell the spirits to go away and leave me alone since, as a teenager, I sometimes found their demands overwhelming and unwelcome – a curse, if you like. I didn't want to know. But then, on the other hand, communicating with them was as natural to me as breathing and I felt a desire to do this work. So I was in a state of denial one minute, acceptance the next and then in a state of turmoil at other times.

2

The Rescue of Souls

Soon after that I began work which involved the rescue of souls – helping spirits move on. This could happen at any time. I could be walking down the street, for example, when I would see – as I did one time – two men standing at a set of traffic lights. I knew they were lost. When I went up to them, I asked them what was wrong. One of them had been killed in a hit-and-run traffic accident and his spirit was trapped. I asked him where he was and he told me he didn't know. Automatically I was able to take him into the Light on his journey. I would normally do this by explaining to them first of all where they were. Some of them really didn't know they were dead, in fact. And they kept wandering, looking for something. So, if they were prepared to go forward to God, I then helped them move on. If they were not, then there was nothing I could do for them.

Some of the spirits I encountered would look like

any average person you would meet on the street. Others wore clothes from different times, as far back as the nineteenth century. And then there were the spirits that looked bloody and battered, with limbs hanging off – usually the result of a terrible accident. I would have to look away in disgust. Yet I always felt I could not turn them away because I felt so sorry for them.

I always saw them in the flesh. They were not hazy or "ghostly". I simply saw them the way I saw any other people. But there was one big difference. They usually had a type of light around them.

But sometimes I saw spirits with a dark light around them and I would look into their eyes and see a blackness. That's when I knew that their souls had been infiltrated by Satan. Immediately, through prayer, I would throw a light of protection around me so they couldn't harm me, but I would always do what I could to help them move on.

Trapped Spirits

When we leave this world for good, some of us, for whatever reason, become trapped and cannot complete the journey into the spirit world. Many of these people tend to have died a violent, quick death and simply don't realise they are dead. They are confused and need direction to help them on their path. Others, who have made their pact with evil, are genuinely terrified. They too cannot move on, because they don't want to, so afraid are they when the realisation that they are dead hits them. If they move on, they know instinctively that they will pass into Hell and eternal damnation. So what do they do? They hang around. They are known as "Earth-bound spirits" and will have passed out of their bodies in total confusion.

These spirits are unclean. They can still be helped but only by those who have a genuine ability to rescue them. And who are protected against Satan. If and when they stay, they can torment the living and can often linger in houses, especially if that's where the death took place. They can see us and they think we can see them and that's why they move things around in houses, turn on light switches, and so on. This is their way of making a statement – this is my house and I'll do things my way. In many instances, they may only be trying to let us know that they need help urgently. If they wish to go into the Light, I can help these spirits. Normally I will call in the angels and my spirit guides to help me move them onwards. But when it is more difficult I have seen Jesus come for them, which reminds me forcibly that He is truly merciful. These spirits are always given a last chance to redeem themselves after death.

On a more sinister level, these spirits, in a last-ditch attempt to avoid moving forward, can manifest themselves in vulnerable people. Some of them are so powerful they can enter a person's spirit and possess them without the person knowing this is happening. It is only later, when their victims start to show outward signs of possession, that their behaviour changes. Very often, without help, these unfortunate people can end up going mad as a direct result of being possessed. These spirits can also kill the person they have infested, although that is rare. But it does happen.

When spirits contact me I always ask them where they come from. They will either say "I come from the Light" or "I come in God's name". If they come from the darkness they try to deceive me first. So they give me roundabout answers. I ask them, "In whose name do you come?" and they might answer "You know, the man that was on the cross." My response to this is to inform them that they are in a place of darkness. I then give them a choice to move on into the Light. In some cases they fall away and don't come back. In other cases they cry. I then help them to ask for God's forgiveness. I tell them that they need to renew their faith and I move them towards the Light. They are in God's hands after that.

A Lost Child

Once, when I was well past my teenage years, I was called to a house where the owners reported incidents of unexplained noises, including the wailing of a child's voice. On entering the house I felt a coldness and a kind of sadness which became more pronounced as I moved upstairs towards the bedroom where the activity was reported.

I looked in the wardrobe and saw a little girl, no more than seven years of age, cowering at the back, wearing a Holy Communion dress.

"What's your name?" I asked her.

"Aisling," she told me.

"What year is it?" I asked her.

She told me it was the year 1975. It was, in fact, many years after that date.

I said to her, "You look beautiful. Your dress is really nice. What happened to you?"

She replied, "I don't know. I am here all the time."

"Are you happy?" I asked.

"Yes."

Then I noticed she seemed to be looking around her for something. "What are you looking for?" I asked her.

"I can't find my doll."

"But your doll is behind you," I told her.

With that, she grabbed the doll and began cuddling it and singing gently to it.

"Aisling," I said to her, "I am going to get a carriage for you, a beautiful carriage. I will get into the carriage with you and will take you to meet the angels."

I lifted her up and gently placed her in the "carriage". I told her not to be afraid, that everything was going to be okay and that the beautiful angels were going to take her into a lovely place. Then with a push I let her go into the Light. The angels then came and took her to heaven. I found out later that this child had died in this particular house just weeks before her First Holy Communion.

Divine Assistance: Angels

The interesting thing I began to notice about my gift, in time, was that I was being helped in my work. I was not alone. I would call in what I now know to be my spirit guides to tell me about the person in front of me, particularly those parts of their lives where their spiritual emptiness had created desperate unhappiness.

Years ago if you told people you saw angels, they would think you stark raving mad. Today they tend to think again before they brand you. Why? Because so many people today are now coming forward admitting that they, too, see angels.

I began to see angels when I reached my early twenties. Some angels appeared as you would expect to see them – with wings. Others looked just like ordinary people. I saw angels first in dreams and then during the day. It started off gently, when I would feel a spirit beside me, guiding me. The spirit guide would stay with me in any situation but would become stronger if, and when, I found myself in any kind of danger. My spirit guide would help me make the right decision, or, for example, help me avoid situations where I would be involved in a row with someone.

Though as a young child I did not associate the spirits I saw with religion, I later always associated my spirit guides and angels with God. They were all part of the one spiritual "other side" to me. I believe that angels are part of God the Almighty Father's Heaven and not from some other planet or parallel universes as we are led to believe by some of today's spiritualists. God is the maker and creator of all things. I will never deviate from this belief. So whatever name people want to give to the spiritual world which I believe in passionately, it all boils down to one thing. God made the universe and the spiritual world is contained within his domain.

But one thing I can assure you: angels do exist; they are real; they are not a figment of people's imagination and they are an important part of our lives. They help to protect us and guide us in our day-to-day lives. But, ideally, we must acknowledge them if we are to receive the graces and benefits they can bring into our lives. It's amazing really, but most people I speak to today who believe in angels, who pray to them and request favours, will tell you that they are never let down.

You must ask your angels to help you. They cannot help you unless you ask. Sounds simple, doesn't it? But they cannot interfere with your free will. They cannot, for example, bestow a gift on you just because they are close to you. That's not the way it works. You must ask to receive.

I continued to do "readings" for people, my aim at all times being to improve the quality of their life through spiritual enlightenment. Now, with the help of my spirit guides and angels, my readings were more profound and more accurate. If the person for whom I was doing the reading told me they had a relationship problem with someone close to them, I would know immediately what the problem was. In fact, I would go beyond the immediate problem and the person before me. For example, if a girl came to me and told me she was having a problem with her boyfriend's moods, I would know straight away what *his* problem related to. It could be a health matter, an addiction problem, or a psychological issue such as depression. I would instantly know. And so I would tell her to make sure her partner acknowledged the problem openly and sought help in order to resolve it.

My spirit guides would always show me the truth. They would also give me signs to prove to the person that I was genuine, for example I would describe someone close to them, their habits, their likes and dislikes and special "traits". The accuracy of each communication was uncanny.

If I was helping a person to communicate with a deceased loved one or vice versa, I would have my spirit guides at my side helping. But, nine times out of ten, I would also invite the spirit guides of the deceased – the ones that they, themselves, had with them when they were alive on Earth – to communicate with the person in front of me. Indeed, sometimes they came uninvited.

For example, take the case of one deceased woman who came through to me so that she could communicate an important message to her daughter. The woman had died one year previously. In life she was unpopular and caused a lot of difficulties in her family through rows, stubborn silences and a refusal to take part in family life. When I saw her the light around her was faint and I knew something was up. It meant she was disturbed and troubled. Then, out of the blue came her own spirit guide who explained to me that this woman was very misunderstood in life. I was told that she had suffered from agoraphobia and had numerous panic attacks that were never discussed in the open. She kept her problems to herself. Her husband could never get her to go anywhere as she wouldn't leave the house. Their marriage suffered as a result. The atmosphere in the house was so bad it impacted badly on the entire family in every way. This spirit guide was encouraging me to explain to the woman's daughter that it wasn't her fault. The woman then came back to pass on her love and peace as well as to ask forgiveness.

I received tremendous satisfaction from these readings. I loved helping people, especially when I would see the joy and peace in their faces afterwards. How I wished that I could have spent my days doing such work! That was not to be the case, though, as I had a living to make and I had to go out and earn my wages. My family had little enough to survive on as it was and my contribution was essential. Besides, in those days there were no such things as "spiritual reading classes". They didn't exist then. I would have been laughed at.

The Gift of Channelling

This is a subject I need to explain to the reader for the purposes of understanding my communications with Our Lady.

I was in my late teens when the fact I had the gift of "channelling" was made abundantly clear to me. I first saw my role simply as one where I had to help spirits move on but my relationship to the spirit world became ever more complex and I realised there were many aspects to it. At times I felt like I was trying to complete a jigsaw and that it was only by placing all the pieces together systematically to form a picture that I could understand.

As I moved into my twenties my "channelling" became even more pronounced and stronger than ever. I found I could "go into channel" really quickly – at the blink of an eye – whereas before it would have taken me up to five or ten minutes and I would have to be in a very quiet environment with no distractions.

So what *is* "channelling"? It means, simply, that you allow spiritual entities to communicate with you and deliver predictions and messages through you. All of us have a spiritual channel but very few of us tap into it. Usually it's because we just don't know how. Often it's because we don't believe it. Anyone can act as a channel but some people, including myself, seem to find it very easy to become attuned. But beware. It doesn't just mean that you receive messages from those that have died on this Earth or those who come from the angelic realm. You could connect with demons.

For those who are not familiar with "spirit channelling" let me explain that when a visionary makes a prediction or delivers a message, it is not he or she who is actually doing that. The visionary is a spiritual connector who is being used as a channel. Imagine a vortex opening up in the top of your head and picture a jug full of messages being poured in like water; that gives you an idea of what it's like. You don't choose the messages, you simply receive them, and you have no control over the process. It is the spirits who tell me what is going on and what is going to happen. They either tell me directly or I receive their messages in a dream. These dreams – unlike ordinary dreams – are extremely clear. I might be shown a future event around a person known or, sometimes, unknown to me. On waking, I remember every single word and write it down. If I ever lose the paper I can easily write it down again, word for word. If you were to compare both papers, you would see the exact same words, even if they were written a few days apart. This is the gift I use when I record Our Lady's messages after she has appeared to me.

I believe that most people have a psychic gift but simply have not opened themselves up to it. In any event, I believe that my own spiritual connection, and my later gift of healing, were all meant to happen for a reason. To work to impart messages for Our Lady.

Clairvoyants – a Warning

Some people have told me I am clairvoyant, whatever that really means. I am not very comfortable with this term, as I believe that there are people in the world working as clairvoyants who can abuse their power. Yet I have psychic gifts – it's a fact and it's not something I am ashamed of. While I realise that there are many good clairvoyants and psychics out there, I worry about the number of people who are being seduced by the whole area of astrology, tarot cards and the use of Ouija boards. Some clairvoyants and mediums may be working on "the other side"– the darkness. I am not saying that all people with psychic gifts abuse their power – some are well-meaning. But it is important to understand one thing: Jesus warned us in the Bible that false prophets present themselves to us in disguise, a little like a wolf in sheep's clothing (Matthew 7:15–20). In the wrong hands, that is mediums or clairvoyants who are not working "in the Light", you could find yourself in trouble.

The biggest threat to people who get sucked into this craze is that by listening to just any clairvoyant and accepting that what they say as true, they can become diverted and lose their real spiritual course. That's what makes Satan so happy. In the Bible, the Second Letter to the Corinthians 11:13–15 says: *"For such are false apostles, deceitful workers, transforming themselves into apostles of Christ. And no marvel; for Satan himself is transformed into an angel of light."*

The term "clairvoyant" is, quite rightly, frowned upon by the Catholic Church. Yet, without even knowing me, this is a stick they have wrongly used to beat me with in my work.

Mediums

This brings me on to another topic – mediums. I viewed the gift of communicating with dead people as directly relating to a natural love of God the Almighty Father. I do not, and never have, considered myself a medium as the term is usually understood. The work of a medium is not necessarily done out of any belief in God or love. This was, in a nutshell, another fundamental difference between me and the organisation in question.

A medium is someone with a gift who deliberately sets out to communicate with a deceased loved one to allow them to reconnect with those left behind. By doing this, they have a responsibility to remain grounded and free from any kind of delusion or opinion. It is their duty, I believe, that when they accept the delivery of a message, it must be rooted in the highest principles of God. Failure to obey the right rules can lead to disaster. They must always ask God and the angels to guide them.

In addition, they must be able to recognise the exact source of their message. They must always learn to differentiate whether or not the message is coming from their own consciousness or from the spiritual realm at all. In all instances, they have a duty to ensure that the message comes with the blessing of a spirit guide given by the loved ones of the person they are working with. Above all, they need to safeguard themselves against souls who come from "the darkness". Therein lies the danger.

Evil spirits can permeate a room very quickly. In the wrong circumstances, and without the correct procedures in place, they can enter a physical body so fast that it may not be obvious at first. That's when the real problems begin. Mediums must be extremely careful, because once evil presents itself, it is very difficult to get rid of it. If you align this practice with other occult practices such as the use of Ouija boards, then it can cause terrible havoc and infestation of a kind that is unimaginable. The only way to rid the person of the possession is through exorcism, which very few people, even including Catholic priests, can manage successfully.

Many innocent people, attending a séance for example – all in the name of a bit of fun – can end up possessed by the Devil and in many cases can end up losing their minds. I have come across this situation time and time again. I cannot emphasise enough the dangers in dabbling in spirit-connection activities without a divine connection with God. This is why I hate it when people call me a medium or a clairvoyant, because I am not. I see myself only as a channel of love, a channel of God with a connection with spirit.

3

Love and Marriage

I met my first serious girlfriend when I was eighteen years of age. I fell in love, hook, line and sinker.

At the time I was working for an asphalt company which had the contracts for a number of schools, hospitals and churches around the country, including new and old buildings. I was a roofer. This job brought me to nearly every single county in Ireland. I would be away from Monday to Friday and home only for the weekend. We could be in Trim, for example, for six weeks and in Dundalk for eight weeks.

Because of all the travelling I had to do, my girlfriend and I spent too much time apart, so after a while we split up.

In 1979 I was involved in an accident at work when I fell from a roof on a construction site in Dublin. I damaged a disc in my lower back. I could barely walk after that and could only shuffle along while I awaited an appointment to have the disc readjusted.

My father died in March 1980 of a massive heart attack, aged only fifty-six. I was heartbroken and found it so hard to accept that I didn't have the stomach to go to Mass. This began a gradual process of turning away from being a practising Catholic, though as my healing and spiritual work involved calling on the Holy Spirit and Our Lady, I still felt a genuine love for her and for God.

Then in April I had to go into St Stephen's hospital to have a four-hour operation on my spine. That helped repair the disc but did not really restore my back so I still suffered badly from back pain. I could not work again after that time.

It was a bad time for me but something good also happened in 1980. I bumped into a girl named Marian Richardson on the street one day. I told her about my father and how I was feeling and she was very sympathetic.

Marian and I went out after that and we fell in love. We were going out for four years before we got married in April 1984 in St Matthew's Church, Ballyfermot. I had applied to get married and was told by a priest, who was younger than me (I was twenty-nine at the time) that I would have to do a pre-marriage course. I said I didn't want to do one. I just wanted to be married in the eyes of God and I couldn't see what this course had to do with that. Besides, what could this celibate priest, who was younger than me, have to tell me about marriage? The parish priest was called and informed me at my home that unless I did a pre-marriage course, he would not marry us. I told him I would write a letter to the Pope and eventually he gave in. I don't know why, but from the start my experience with representatives from the Catholic Church has not been good.

We settled down in a house in Ballyfermot. We had five children. Our first-born, Daniel James, unfortunately died during the birth from complications. Marian was suffering from a very bad dose of pneumonia. She never saw the baby because she was so ill. I told the nurse that I was up the walls over my wife. "Will you make sure you bury my child's body in the Angels' Plot in Glasnevin?" I begged her. But I don't know if he was buried there.

This plot is the resting place for over fifty thousand babies, most but not all of whom were stillborn. Glasnevin, an interdenominational cemetery established by the great Daniel O'Connell in 1832, was one of the few cemeteries in the past that allowed unbaptised babies to be buried in consecrated ground.

In those days when a woman had a stillborn baby or when a baby died during the birth, the mother never saw that baby. The body was not normally given back to the parents for burial. Daniel James's body was never given back to us and we were never provided with a birth certificate – only a death certificate.

Many years later, a scandal emerged because the parents of such children were not routinely informed of their loved ones' organs being retained by many hospitals throughout the country. The matter was, and still is, being fought by the group Parents for Justice, of which I am a member.

I will never forget him. How could I? This beautiful child, Daniel James, has since gone up to the spirit world and he is with me every day of my life. I see him today in my visions as a young adult in his early twenties. And he is close to me the entire time.

After the death of Daniel James, I went through a rough time and I'm afraid I blamed God for my misfortune. I had begun to attend the odd Mass again by this time but now I stopped. Nor did I go to Confession.

The Turning Point – the Day I Died

In January 1986 I was trying to get down the stairs in my house when I fell to the bottom and severely crushed my ankle. It was termed a "parachute ankle injury". My leg swelled to twice its size and, in excruciating agony, I was rushed into hospital, where I was sent straight to surgery.

I will never forget that experience.

On the operating table in St James's Hospital, Dublin, I was given an anaesthetic to knock me out. The only problem was, while I should have lost consciousness, I hadn't. I found myself floating slowly upwards outside of my body. Drifting until it seemed as if I was suspended from the ceiling. I was in the top right-hand corner in the room as I watched, fascinated, while the doctors in their gowns worked on my body. I couldn't see my face or my body, as it was covered up with a green sheet while they operated. Confused, I looked at the table and wondered whether I was dreaming. Or maybe hallucinating? I was puzzled. What was I doing here? Why was I looking down at myself? Was it a dream?

As I floated, I felt a sudden pulling. Then I could hear a deep loud rumbling noise, as if a fast river was rushing by. The noise got louder and louder, filled with a type of echo. Then there was a feeling of being propelled upwards with a great energy, body upright, head up, legs straight. I felt like I was in an elevator made for one person, with no sides or top, and I was moving rapidly. Rushing on now at tremendous speed, my body felt weightless, light as a feather. I was filled with a mix of fear, wonder, curiosity and fascination. Looking back, I have often described it as the nearest feeling to what it must be like when you are being born. And I suppose that's what it was – a form of birth, a rebirth.

At the very top, I saw a huge bright dazzling misty light. I then seemed to be standing in a mystical gigantic cave with never-ending walls in the distance, an open expanse of some sort.

Looking around, I was dumbstruck. I was filled at first with a sense of awe. Speechless, I looked around, amazed to see so many thousands and thousands of angels, of every size, shape and colour imaginable. *So, so many – how could there be so many?* I thought. I never believed it possible that so many angels could actually exist. They were everywhere. And they were happy, smiling, and full of life and joy. Their light, so bright and dazzling, which seemed to blend into the sun, enveloped me. This sun had a surreal, larger-than-life, dazzling beauty that seemed to span out for thousands of miles, never-ending. There were flowers everywhere, but they were unlike any flowers I have ever seen before. The array of colours and shapes were not the only unusual thing but the way in which they seemed to float was mesmerising.

It was then that I noticed a man standing waiting for me. It was my father, Seán, with a beautiful little boy around two years of age. Amazed and thrilled to see my father again, it was only when I looked more closely at the little boy that it all began to make sense. My heart flipped over when I realised, without being told, that this was, in fact, my beautiful baby son Daniel James, who had died during birth. But now he appeared to me as a little boy. He looked at me and somehow seemed to recognise me. I couldn't believe it. I noticed then that he was holding onto the hand of my father who, in turn, held onto his little hand tightly and protectively. They both looked so contented and at peace and their happy smiling faces gave me a sense of such huge comfort. I felt ready now to move on.

Suddenly everything became quiet, calm and still.

The angels all seemed to be looking beyond at something or someone. Then the colour of the light and the atmosphere seemed to be changing to layers of light with a starry quality. It became even more pronounced and more breathtakingly beautiful than before. Then a tall handsome figure of a beautiful man stepped out of the light. My heart was filled with a sense of hope and urgency. The indescribable love, humility and pleasure I felt instantly cannot ever be put into words. It's impossible. I felt not one ounce of fear. Nothing but pure, absolute love permeated every inch of my being. I was in total ecstasy. It was exhilarating. Then I was taken by the hand and welcomed into Heaven by Jesus Christ. He embraced me and held me in his arms. I had come home at last. I was at peace at last. I relaxed and began to take everything in.

One angel stood out from the rest and got my attention. He was much taller than the other angels. I knew instinctively that I was looking at Michael the Archangel. He was in charge of the other angels. He held a large silver sword and looked powerful and majestic. All the other angels seemed to look up to him and honour him. I felt a strange kind of affinity with him and from that time I have a very special devotion to this powerful angel, whose role is to free us from fear and provide us with the courage to fight evil. He is with me the whole time and offers me complete protection and safety from physical danger of any kind, which I face, almost daily, from the Evil One.

Then to my absolute delight and joy I saw Our Lady, the Blessed Mother of Jesus Christ, Queen of Heaven. She was glowing in her full heavenly glory, beaming at me with the most loving, gentlest of smiles. Her beauty was startling. Young, with long thick dark hair, she wore a dazzling gown in shimmering layers that appeared to be made from a soft silky material in a multitude of soft, pale but exotic shades, the colours of which do not exist on Earth. Highly revered in Heaven, she is Queen of All the Angels and has a very powerful role.

Suddenly, I felt a spirit permeate every part of my body and fill me with love, joy, confidence, excitement and peace. I know now that this was the Holy Spirit. I felt at total peace. I was excited, like a child. I felt like a baby basking in my mother's arms – that it the best way to describe it – without a care in the world.

The other thing I was fascinated to see is that while we are spirits, we take on a physical body and it is usually the body we had at the time of life when we were most happy or at our peak. But we don't speak the way we do on Earth. We don't speak with our voices, we speak with our minds, and we seem to be able to communicate much faster, more efficiently and with complete ease. We are completely aware of who we were on Earth and who we were in spirit before we were born on Earth. You see, we all begin as spirits. Then we are born. Then we return as spirits again. So, who we were on Earth, once we are in Heaven doesn't really matter that much. Yet some spirits will deliberately hold on to their memories of Earth, particularly if they had a deep love for someone. Our memories are intact and we can hold onto memories if we want. However, most of those who pass over don't necessarily want to hold onto these memories because they are so happy in the spirit world. We know who our loved ones are – both on Earth and in the afterlife – but we accept that we have moved on and now have a new world in which we exist and it's a world that is nowhere like the Earth. It is far superior. Earth pales into insignificance when compared with Heaven. The single biggest difference, apart from the sheer beauty and magnificence of Heaven, is the love you feel. No love on Earth is as strong or as palpable. The love we share on Earth is good and it's important, but it is only a shimmer of what pure love is in God's Kingdom.

My full memory still remained. I just couldn't believe it. I had no blank spots. I knew exactly who I was. I knew I had just died. But I wasn't afraid. In fact, I was bursting with happiness. And why wouldn't I be?

So here I was in the company of Jesus Christ. He made me see that love is extremely powerful and that we must love others as we love ourselves. Without the light of God in our lives, we are unlikely to feel real love or any meaningful long-lasting love. If we seek out love in others, we will feel the Light of God.

It was then that I was taken by the angels into a room where I was made acutely aware of all the events that had taken place in my life up until then. I was shown my life in what looked like a movie being played out before me – in full technicolour! So fast and furious did it pan out that it reminded me of one of those old-fashioned movie reels, spinning and spinning, faster and faster, churning out reams and reams of film footage. Shocked, I looked and saw the hundreds and hundreds of deeds and events of my life, down to the smallest detail, flash before me. I was made aware of everything I remembered. Not one deed went unheeded. I could see clearly all the good things I did in my life and felt proud. Yet I could see, too, with complete clarity, all the flaws in my life up to that age and the injuries I caused others either directly or indirectly. All were laid bare. Immediately I understood. I knew I was being given a chance to re-evaluate the way I was living my life and to come back and rectify what I was doing wrong. I was full of remorse.

We are judged in Heaven on our selfishness on Earth; our greed; our treatment of others; our lust for worldly goods; self-ego; idolatry of false gods and people whom we place on pedestals; lack of belief in God the Father; disrespect for God. All the terrible sins we are guilty of are exposed in their raw ugliness. Sins that we sadly, but mistakenly, believed didn't really exist at all, that didn't really matter. Unfortunately, they did, and they do. This realisation hit me so forcibly. It was a shocking revelation.

I was also shown the truth, the simple truth. While our spirits are contained within our bodies on Earth, the spirit does not die at the point of physical death. No, the spirit remains alive after we die. It never, ever dies. It doesn't die in Heaven. It doesn't die in purgatory. It doesn't die in Hell. It remains forever. And so, how we live our lives on Earth will dictate our future in the next life. Sadly, not all spirits return to Heaven. I learned that Earth is a testing ground for spirits within the human body. If spirits/souls manage to survive the struggle on Earth, through love of one another, believe in a superior God and deny evil and sin, they will find their way back to God. While God is merciful, souls that choose not to follow the truth make their own Hell. They choose Hell because that is what they want. This makes God very sad and he will do everything he can to save our souls. But those who end up in Hell choose this willingly. They fall victim to the Evil One but do nothing to redeem themselves afterwards. And so they are doomed. God is merciful and does give them a second chance after death when they are brought into the Light, but those who have allied themselves with the Evil One often choose not to take this second chance. It's by their own free will. And God cannot and does not interfere with people's own free will.

Those who have near-death experiences are luckier than others because they have a chance to redeem themselves back on Earth to prepare for death. They have the advantage that they know what to expect! The one thing about a near-death experience is that those who come back change completely. They lose all fear of death and develop a deeper love of God.

Suddenly I felt I was moving backwards. All the images around me began to fade. I was being propelled backwards at an alarming speed, into a dark tunnel, like I was on a looped rollercoaster. The light faded rapidly and I fell spinning into total darkness.

As I looked around me I knew I was in a bright room. I felt a wall behind me and could see a crowd of people below me. I knew then that I was back in the operating theatre. I looked down and saw doctors standing around a figure on a trolley. Puzzled, I looked at the person on the trolley and realised frantically that it was me. I began to panic, because I felt myself moving towards the body. I could feel myself entering this body and immediately felt a sense of heaviness and excruciating pain. Feelings of electric jolts raged through my body and I felt myself jerk uncontrollably, as if I was being given electric shocks. Opening my eyes slowly and painfully, I could hear a nurse's voice.

"Come on, Joe, wake up," I heard her say. "You're going into the recovery room."

As I struggled to regain consciousness, I felt a sense of utter dread and hopelessness. I was horrified, shocked and bitterly disappointed that I had to come back into this body. *Oh God, no*, I thought. *How could this be happening? Why did I have to come back?* I screamed silently, but to no avail.

∾ ∾

After this operation, I realised I could never undertake physical work of any kind again. I was virtually disabled from the previous injury to my spine and now my ankle was shattered too. Even walking was difficult for me and I couldn't stand for any extended time. Sitting for any length of time in an upright chair caused dreadful discomfort.

However, my injuries changed my life for the better in many ways. That's when I realised, with absolute clarity, that I now had a real cross in life to bear. My devotion to Our Lady increased and I developed a strong affinity with God the Almighty Father.

Immediately after this I began to attend Mass again. However, I prayed in my own way rather than reciting well-known prayers which in fact I had forgotten. It wasn't until my visit to Medjugorje in 2009 that I began to receive the Sacraments on a regular basis. However, I would like to make it clear that as soon as my children were old enough they were brought to Mass every Sunday – we never missed it as a family.

My Life after Death

4

Spiritual Healing

After my near-death experience, I felt a massive urge to develop my faith and was drawn towards Christian spirituality in a way that I hadn't experienced before. I felt a constant restless urge to help people, living and dead with their spiritual well-being. Having long ago accepted my natural gift of spiritual connection, I now felt I needed to expand on my gift and hone my skills in communicating with spirits. That's when I decided to join a well-known organisation for spiritual healers in Ireland.

I was the first person in Ireland to receive a FÁS (National Training and Employment Authority) Grant for a course in a spiritual healing centre. During the three years I spent there, studying how to communicate with and rescue spirits, I learned a lot. However, the first thing I realised was that there was a fundamental difference between my approach and the beliefs of those who ran the centre. Their organisation was not associated in any way with the love of God, the Almighty Father, which meant they did not see the source of spiritual healing as “divine”, which is exactly what I believe it to be.

So a conflict arose between me and the organisation in question over my belief that God was the power behind any spiritual activity. While I believed that Jesus was responsible for spirit rescue and that Michael the Archangel protected me during this work, members of the association had a difficulty with this. They believed in the spiritual world but didn’t necessarily believe that it was connected with God or religion. The difference with me was that when I went into “channel” during the rescue of souls, it was Jesus and the angels who helped me bring the spirits to the Light. I am not saying that their approach was completely wrong; it just pains me that they didn’t “get it”!

However, I did enjoy my time there and learned how to hone and define my skills around the gifts I had. For example, for me meditation came naturally – I never had to work on it. So, while I could always meditate instantaneously, they taught me how to meditate in a certain way. The way they taught was to sit down and close your eyes, let your mind wander and let the spirit take over. They taught me how to do the special breathing that is required and how to call your spirit guides in. This was very beneficial and seemed to be quite powerful. It was a new approach for me and it certainly helped me communicate with the spirit world. It was different to the way in which I was used to going into channel, but it was very interesting.

Before my accident I had always believed, and fully accepted, that I was different to other people. It was as if I felt I had a job to do that had some kind of higher purpose. But I was restless, confused and needed clarification as to what exactly I was, what my gifts really meant. I needed to meet other people with similar gifts and I wanted to know how they worked. So my time in the centre was inspiring. I felt comfortable that I was with other people who had the gift of spiritual connection.

However, I parted ways with the organisation. I believed these gifts came from God. They believed they were the ones in real control. I thought that was nonsense.

5

Satan, "The Deceiver", Exposed

People laugh when you mention Satan, "The Devil", "The Evil One" or "The Deceiver" – whatever name you want to give him. They don't really believe he exists. He's just part of old folklore, a figment of people's imagination. In the modern, sophisticated, intellectually and technologically advanced world that we live in today, surely the idea of the Devil is just superstitious nonsense?

But he's very real, and he's everywhere in the world today. His biggest talent lies in convincing people he doesn't really exist. I call him "The Deceiver" because this is the name given to him by Our Lady. He convinces people that the existence of God is not real. That the truth is a lie. He blinds the minds of people.

Once a beautiful angel of God, the Deceiver became a fallen angel, leading him to organise a revolt which resulted in a battle in Heaven. His single goal now is to destroy the human race and claim the world as his own. He works harder than ever before to win over souls – the souls of many unsuspecting people who, through ignorance, don't believe he exists. This is not an accident. It is all due to the fact that he needs as many souls as he can snare before the Second Coming of Jesus Christ on Earth.

He delights in spreading lies about God amongst those who lack belief in God in the first instance. Unfortunately, his schemes are succeeding. And today he is very organised.

You only have to look around the world today to see the strange, weird and frightening religious cults which have sprung up. Behind their façades lies the Deceiver's work. Many of these cults are satanic cults but are dressed in "sheep's clothing". Some of them are open and honest in their beliefs. That's okay. They are entitled to their beliefs and make no bones about it. Some, however, are more secretive and much more dangerous.

His goal is to destroy God's relationship with mankind and he sets out, with every chance he gets, to blind the minds of unbelievers from seeing the Light of God. He is the exact opposite of the truth. So everything he achieves – and he is successful – is based on lies.

How he Attacks

The Deceiver's attacks are so subtle, and dressed in respectable, plausible, calm, logical thinking, that his victims don't even realise they are being targeted. So how do you recognise the signs? First of all, he will attack the relationship you have with God. He convinces non-believers that Christians are unsophisticated, ignorant, mad or even psychotic. They, the non-believers, then unwittingly become mouth-pieces for him. I am not suggesting for one minute that people who are non-believers are bad. Not at all. I believe that they have simply moved away from any kind of belief in the afterlife or in supernatural occurrences for various reasons. Many non-believers don't bother to confront the believers because it doesn't interest them to do this. It's not important enough to them to argue the case.

However, it is the active atheist groups, that set out deliberately to undermine Christianity that bother me the most. Their approach is highly aggressive and hidden behind very carefully couched logical debate. Surely, they claim, because the supernatural cannot be proven by scientific means, there can be no "evidence" to support a belief in God? Yet for all their scientific babble they still cannot prove that God doesn't exist. Or that the supernatural isn't real.

Certain atheists, including world-renowned authors and leaders of atheist groups, and I am sorry to say this, also tend to display a certain arrogance that I find deeply offensive. Although, again, just like Christians, they are entitled to their opinion, I suspect that they are trying too hard. It begs the question: are they, in fact, setting up a new religion of their own? I believe this is Satan at his best and most devious. He flirts with and is deeply attracted to the powerful, the intellectual, the successful, political leaders, those in power and, above all the scientists who he can rely on every time to try to prove that God doesn't exist.

Some atheists, who work for organisations set up to promote their views professionally, go to great lengths to undermine every belief in God or spirituality, by pulling people who believe in God apart through scornful ridicule. Much of this is done in such a belittling way it can take your breath away. Christian beliefs are first of all cleverly "gently scolded", with such convincing rational thinking that it can be hard for Christians to fight back. Trying ferociously, at every opportunity, to undermine the Christian faith, they actively strive to prove that the Christian argument is totally absurd. I have seen many attempts by them to ensure that the believer is made to appear simple, ignorant and even downright stupid. "Holiness is a form of madness," is a favourite stick they use to beat Christians with. Then difficult questions are posed where Christians are challenged in a way that questions the very essence of their faith. "Surely you are not suggesting that only those who believe in God are good? Are you saying the rest of us are bad? Isn't this dangerous thinking? Can't it spark off hatred of one another?" Jesus teaches us through his words and acts that it is wrong to judge others in any way. It is for God to judge them and only God knows the human heart.

The Game

Man's quest for happiness and urge to acquire worldly goods is another route by which Satan infiltrates souls. As for the vulnerable people he eventually succeeds in infesting, they then convince themselves that, even in the course of an evil deed, they are "doing good", they are doing the "right thing" in the circumstances they find themselves and, so, they then justify the act by whatever means possible.

The reason Satan places so much emphasis on money is to prey on people's disappointment when they feel that faith can't put bread on the table. The argument he puts before you is cunningly simple. If God is meant to supply you with all your needs in this world, and if you have no money, then he is not doing a good job, is he? So then the game begins. The Deceiver gets people to become addicted to money.

Satan uses the search for wealth to infest people. One of his favourite tactics is to get people to spend as much of their time as possible focusing on money or lack of it! Satan wants money to become people's number one priority in this world. I am not suggesting for a minute that money is evil. Of course not. We all need it to live. Even when we receive it in abundance, this is not a bad thing either. It is only when money is set up as the number one goal to the detriment of everything and everyone around you – when nothing else counts – that you have to worry. It is when it becomes an obsession to the point where the pursuit of it causes absolute destruction to those around you that it becomes perilous. It is here that the Deceiver can be clearly seen to work.

He convinces people that they, and they alone, have the power to attract financial abundance into their lives. They can attain real power, almost divine power, through their positive attitude and ambitious hard work. They are blindly driven to believe that they can achieve anything they set their minds to. You only have to look at the number of books published in recent years to understand that this approach to life has swept people, from every walk of life, right off their feet. While I am a great believer in positive thinking and the powerful energy it brings into people's lives, there is a form of positive thinking that really only amounts to wishful thinking. Promoting the message "You can do anything – achieve the impossible – attract huge wealth into your life with the right frame of mind" has provoked a kind of mass hysteria in recent years. This is where people become convinced that they really are in total charge of their own lives.

However, some of this philosophy taps into a form of spiritualism where you can wish for something and think about it, send out the right vibes and it will happen. What you give out comes back. Yes, there's truth in this but it can only happen if asked for through Divine Grace. This is simply another form of prayer. So that's okay in my view. "Ask and you will receive."

However, it is when people begin thinking that they and only they are in control of how they can attract wealth that when it can become very dangerous. This kind of thinking can lead people into terrible debt where they take unimaginable risks. Buy a luxury and it will attract other luxuries. This thinking has become an obsession in recent years and it basically boils down to one thing only – pure greed.

What happens then is that people can become addicted to gambling – gambling in every sense, such as investing huge sums of money they don't have in schemes that promise to make them huge returns. It is no different to gambling in a game of poker, or losing your family home or all your possessions in a casino.

I believe that the wealth people accumulated in the world over the last decade and which ended in total disaster was, in fact, part of Satan's ultimate plan. People's dreams of acquiring wealth, worrying about money, and cheating others to get their hands on it, results in the inevitable. You get physically ill. You are up to your neck in massive debt which you'll never be able to repay. Marriages and relationships break down. People cheat to worm their way out of the hole they've created for themselves. They'll even resort to murder in some cases.

Then there are the relationships we have with each other in this world. Not only does the Deceiver raise doubts in people's minds about God, but he also makes them challenge their relationships with other people. Other little tricks of his are to convince you, when you are going through a tough time in your life, that other people are to blame. So you end up fighting with them. Oh, how he loves this! This is one of his most classic forms of attack, because he wants people to hate each other. He works to cause havoc around people you love. While God works in an orderly fashion – all things are in order – Satan does the exact opposite.

Another one of Satan's favourite tactics, and one well documented in the Bible, is that he uses guilt as a method to get people to believe that they are bad and that God couldn't love them, especially when they have not lived a good life. When anything goes wrong in their life, he will convince them that God is punishing them. That's when people stop believing in God and push him out of their lives.

One of the most sinister forms of Satan's attacks is when he preys on the bereaved. He attacks people who are grieving the death of a loved one and especially those people who are naturally more "open" spiritually. And, especially, people with a strong faith in God. The first thing he does is present an image of the deceased, usually a very happy image, to make you believe that they have come back to you. To tell you everything is okay. This kind of vision, and one you hear reported of quite a lot, is comforting. Then he can get you to believe what the vision is telling you and very often the bereaved is taken aback by the request.

It may seem so much out of character and unlike the person you knew and loved when they were alive. They can be used to plant ideas, thoughts and very negative thinking – all designed to infest you and your beliefs. Usually, the ultimate objective is to encourage the person to take action of some sort that is against the person's Christian faith. And, of course, it is not the spirit of the loved one at all.

Even though he seduces people, and wins them over, the Deceiver really hates us. His hatred for the human race, when he tries to separate them from God and all things good, has only one goal in mind: to ensnare them in his own power. It's because of him that the world is in a chaotic state today and he is, unfortunately, getting stronger all the time. But, the good news is that, although he has huge powers, they are nothing compared to his Creator, God the Almighty Father. He is in fact powerless against God and the angels.

The More Serious Attacks

It's when you actively work with God and the Light, as I do, that you become a primary target of Satan. During the course of my work with Our Lady, I have been attacked by Satan many times, both mentally and physically, during the day and especially at night. These attacks are very distressing. I have been pulled from my bed at night. He has tried to choke me. He has even tried to pull the cross I always wear from around my neck and I have been thrown to the ground as I have prayed. Having spoken to other people who are directly involved with working for God in areas such as healing, I know that they have similar experiences.

Another way he attacks me is through my dreams. In my dreams he often places hideous images before me – half-human half-beast-like figures who he threatens will eat me if I don't follow him. He himself usually comes to me as a beast of some kind. The head he has on him has no relevance to the body and it tends to be half-human half-animal. Sometimes he has a dog's head and he drools when he looks at me.

Then he promises me the most wonderful rich and wealthy life if I pull away from my work with God and work for him. He is extremely persuasive. But I have learned to wake myself up out of my dreams quickly. At times I have woken up with marks and bruising on my ribs and lower body and legs and red lines in the shape of claw-marks under my skin. Very often he shows me huge flames about thirty feet high and then tries to surround me with them. He can never for some reason touch me with the flames.

He has only one message for me and it's the same one time and time again. He makes it very clear to me that he wants me to stop doing any work for God. Then come the promises: he always tells me that he will grant me anything and everything that I could wish for in this life if I stop working for the Light. Then, as for the curses that come out of him! You may think, in this world, we are immune to cursing because we hear it so often. But, believe you me, the curses that come out of this creature are vile and so disgusting I could never put them into print. The names he gives to Jesus, for example, are so abominable they are worse than anything you would hear in this life or believe possible. Another image he reveals to me is that of little babies, just new born. Then in front of me he tears them apart as they scream out in bloodcurdling agony. He pulls their heads off and transfixes my stare so that I cannot look away.

Then in other dreams it's the exact opposite. He adopts a different approach. It can take the form of a beautiful happy dream. One time he showed me the Earth from above, floating. I could see the lovely colours. "This is all yours, Joe, if you come and work for me with my power." And when I say no, the dream stops immediately.

I looked in his eyes once and saw that they are a mix of red and black. If he stares at you long enough you can go into a hypnotic state and he can convince you to do anything. Which is why I now never look into his eyes. Every time an encounter happens I am deeply distressed for at least a week afterwards.

Other experiences I have had at the hands of the Deceiver are told in more detail later in the book, when I describe what happened after the apparitions of Our Lady began and when I became a more serious target for the Evil One.

It frightens me when I hear people say they don't believe in Satan, that no, he doesn't exist. But let me assure you that Satan is very powerful. In extreme cases, which I will explain later, he can even kill you.

Protection from Satan

I always try to explain to people, especially non-believers, that they must always be on their guard against the Deceiver and learn how to protect themselves.

Persistent, relentless, scheming, patient, cunning and a liar, he will stop at nothing to win over your soul. But you can protect yourself in many ways. The first thing of course is to consider avoidance! Avoid tarot cards and Ouija boards and any form of occult practices. The problem with Ouija boards is that they really work! They were originally used to contact departed relatives or friends. Now nearly all the entities associated with the Ouija boards are of the evil variety. If one of the golden rules about playing the Ouija board is to "Never ask about God" (for fear of the anger it will bring into your home), you can be assured that you are dealing with a dangerous piece of witchcraft.

Young people and groups of friends holding evening parties all think them harmless fun, without realising the dangers. The dabblers who haven't a clue what they are doing end up engaging with an evil spirit voluntarily. The evil spirit can attach itself to you, your mind, and very often the home in which the "game" is being played. Once exposed to an evil spirit your life will not be the same afterwards. I know of a number of cases, including that of one young woman in her twenties, who literally lost her mind. She was institutionalised for twenty years and is only now becoming stable. Not only that but I have been asked by a number of people from around the world to help their loved ones who have been damaged beyond medical help through participating in the occult through Ouija boards.

Finally, the evil spirits that are released from Ouija boards, if they are not dealt with firmly, can affect your life negatively for many years to come.

6

Exorcisms

I have, on occasion, been asked to perform exorcisms, where it has become evident that someone has become possessed by Satan.

You may well ask, how does a lay person like me end up carrying out exorcisms? Why don't I leave it to the priests? It is the dire lack of available Catholic priests willing, or qualified, to handle exorcisms that lead people to call on me. Working to fight Satan leaves you exposed to his attacks – for life. It is not something you jump into willingly. But my love of God and my devotion to help salvage souls from his evil clutches means now that I can never turn back.

Even though satanic possessions are on the increase, we don't have the priests to deal with them. We desperately need more priests, more exorcists. This applies all over the world. Sadly, the Catholic Church has been very slow to appoint them. Also, even though priests are qualified, through the

Sacrament of Holy Orders, they still need permission from their bishop to handle exorcisms. This leaves many poor souls exposed and vulnerable to Satan.

The Catholic Church, in response to the Second Vatican Council, attempted to modernise itself, at least in so far as it fairly quickly discounted old medieval practices, including exorcisms. They played them down to such an extent that many priests stopped believing in the Devil's existence. Pope John Paul II, who himself performed three exorcisms during his twenty-three-year reign, responded differently. He knew that Satan's power was on the increase and demonic possession was infiltrating modern society.

Certain priests have accused me of tampering in this work. They claim that they, and only they, can perform an exorcism. Well, that's not quite true. But there is a difference between a lay person's role in an exorcism and that of a Catholic priest.

In my case – and I must emphasise this – I act as a facilitator, where Jesus Christ is the mediator – not me. I'm just a channel. Where a Catholic priest performs the exorcisms, he stands in for Christ and so himself becomes the mediator. It is he who exorcises the sins of the victim to defeat Satan. I, on the other hand, *call in the mediator* – Jesus Christ. I act in his name.

In order to perform an exorcism, the priest needs the authority passed down from the bishop. When a lay person takes on the task, it is recommended that they go to Confession, or say the Act of Contrition out loud. Ideally, they should receive the Holy Eucharist and attend Mass beforehand to seek God's help.

This unusual, important gift that I have been blessed with has been born out of my love for God, his Son Jesus Christ, the Holy Spirit and Our Blessed Mother, Mary, Mother of God. When I set out to drive out evil spirits, I do it all in the name of Jesus. I believe passionately in the Lord our God and I know that he and all his angels work through me.

I should now make it absolutely clear that at no time do I ever confuse my role with that of a Catholic priest. I would never be so presumptuous. I simply ask Jesus to be present and ask him for a miracle to deliver the victim from the snares of Satan. Any priest who condemns my work needs to look at the scripture in which Jesus, himself, refers to laymen who undertake exorcisms.

> *John said to him* [Jesus], *"Teacher, we saw someone casting out demons in your name, and we tried to stop him, because he was not following us." But Jesus said, "Do not stop him, for no one who does a mighty work in my name will be able soon afterward to speak evil of me. For the one who is not against us is for us."*
>
> *Mark 9:38–40*

Those Most Vulnerable to Satan

So why do satanic possessions take place? Who are the victims? And what have they done to deserve this?

Without generalising too much, there are three types of typical victims.

The first is people who dabble in the occult, partake in satanic rituals, play with Ouija boards and other stupid, dangerous games. Then, suddenly, they find that they have opened themselves up to oppression by the Evil One and other evil spirits. It takes very little time for Satan or his evil army to manifest in the body. But when he does, it is very, very hard to go back to life as you knew it.

Then you have the person who makes a deliberate pact with the Devil, who sells their soul to him. They do this clearly in the knowledge of what they are doing.

Finally you have the vulnerable – those very young souls who are wide open to satanic attacks, and these include children, even babies, at times. While the Devil can manifest himself in people who "invite him in", either deliberately or unwittingly, he can also enter into the spirit of the vulnerable.

Demonic Invasion of Baby "Robert"

I must now jump ahead in time to 2008 to recount the story of Baby "Robert". The day I was asked to perform an exorcism on a two-year-old boy seemed just like any other day. I was in my little prayer room, located over a local florist, which I had opened as a spiritual healing centre in 2006. I was just about to blow out the candles in front of the statue of Our Blessed Mother when the phone rang. I had only finished reciting the Holy Rosary at three o'clock. It was then, for the second time in my life that I was asked to perform an exorcism. The first time involved a teenage boy the year before, which was a mild affair – exorcisms are not all dramatic, in fact they can be low-key affairs.

The father of the little boy had already phoned me three times, desperately pleading with me to rid his son of what he believed to be demonic possession. I tried to get him to consider other options. This time, though, as soon as I heard his voice I knew that circumstances had taken a dramatic turn for the worse.

The names in the following account are not the actual names of the family concerned.

"Joe, it's Brian again! Robert's getting worse!" the voice cried. "We're scared, really scared. I'm sick to the pit of my stomach. Neither of us can sleep. It's too dangerous. We can't leave him even for a moment in case he attacks the baby. Hannah is exhausted and has to hold the baby in her arms now most of the time, in case he bites her. I think he's trying to kill her, I really do," he sobbed.

I stood, phone clenched in my hand, deeply saddened. *Christ*, I thought, closing my eyes, *help me.*

Robert, just two years of age, had been acting strangely for about six weeks. From the start he behaved very badly around his baby sister. At first they put it down to jealousy – to be expected with the arrival of a new baby in the family. But then Robert would try to hurt the baby deliberately – every chance he got. It began with pinching. Sneaky little pinches. His chubby little fingers would sink into the soft plump flesh of his little sister's arm. His mother Hannah would spend forever trying to prise his fingers away, so strong was he, while he would beat his mother furiously with his tiny fist. It was only, though, when Robert began biting the baby, like a vicious dog, that it finally dawned on Brian. Something sinister and completely out of character was at play. Something bad had taken over their lives. The first time Brian asked me to perform an exorcism, I felt it was premature. Instead I told him to take the child to see a doctor. "Brian, I would guess it's just a phase – they call it the 'terrible twos'. Just get him to a doctor," I advised him. "He might refer you to a child psychologist."

Although I had driven out demons as well as evil spirits from places, as well as finding myself in direct face-to-face confrontation with Satan, I knew that to perform an exorcism can be a dangerous mistake if the condition is a medical one.

Exorcism, an ancient practice, is only ever considered as a last resort. It is not something that is done lightly. In the past, when exorcisms were more common, people sometimes confused psychiatric illness, or even epilepsy, with demonic possession. And they still do – even today.

But Brian did just as I instructed him. He took the little boy to see a doctor, who found nothing wrong with him medically. Naturally, of course, the doctor dismissed any notion of demonic possession. Nor did he consider recommending that he see a psychologist. Instead, he suggested that the child be punished the next time he tried to harm his sister and that the parents exert a firmer hand!

Brian continued, "Joe, I don't know how to say this, but his eyes look black – they're not blue any more. He looks at me with . . . how can I put it . . . not just hate in his eyes . . . it's as if he's laughing at us. This child is not my son, Joe. I know it. It's a demon. God help us!"

Filled with dread, I was almost afraid to ask the next question. "Brian, have you noticed anything else? Think carefully."

In a frantic voice, he told me, "He's talking in different languages – weird languages – I don't know what they are – and he's cursing. For God's sake, he can't talk so how can he know these things? Joe, the filth that's coming out of his mouth, it's sickening. You wouldn't believe it. It's shocking." Brian began sobbing uncontrollably at this stage.

I felt my mouth go dry. Straight away, I knew the truth. One of the classic signs of diabolical possession is speaking in different languages and accents. Then there's the obscenities that the unfortunate victims, in their normal lives, would have little knowledge of. Finally I was convinced. This was, without doubt, a genuine case of satanic possession.

"Brian," I said hurriedly, "can you come and collect me?" It was vital to get to the child, and quickly. He agreed and I gave him the address and directions to get there.

I knew that I had to spend time slowly and carefully preparing in advance. First of all, I knelt down and prayed. I asked Michael the Archangel to help me with my work. Then, of course, I said the Holy Rosary, one of the most powerful secret weapons against Satan. He burns every time you say it. If it were to be said enough times in the world, as it should be, then Satan would be destroyed for good. It's *that* powerful. It's both a prayer and a form of meditation to the Blessed Mother of God, the Virgin Mary, and the Holy Trinity.

I then set about quietly gathering my special "tools" needed to help drive out this demon. I gathered my wooden crucifix which features a beautiful silver engraving of Jesus Christ, a bottle of holy water, a miraculous medal blessed by a consecrated priest, my rosary beads, the Holy Bible, rose incense – and, believe it or not, a CD of the famous Marian hymn, the *Ave Maria*. Nowadays, I also use the very special holy oil given me by an exorcist priest, which offers extraordinary protection against the Evil One. I also take with me three white candles, because when lit they attract power, energy and light into a room. When you light rose-scented incense, the demons don't like the smell. There are a lot of different scents they find abhorrent but rose, the sign associated with Our Lady, is the one they hate the most. Our Lady is Satan's mightiest foe and he's terrified of her. That's why the Rosary is so important.

Exorcism can be extremely dangerous, not just for the victim but for the exorcist, and so I knew that I had to be careful in the type of protection I was taking with me. Yet I knew that not only can Satan hurt you physically, he can even kill you, especially during the solemn ritual of an exorcism. That is one of the reasons so few priests volunteer for this service.

When I was ready I knelt and prayed until Brian finally arrived. Very little conversation took place during the drive. Both of us were lost in our own thoughts. Anticipation of what was to come was foremost in our minds. When we eventually got there, I took the holy water out and asked Brian to carry my bag. Walking towards the house, I quickly said a special prayer and sprinkled holy water on the front door as we entered the hallway.

As soon as I walked into the kitchen, I felt a horrible atmosphere that was not only forceful but cold, dark and dank with an underlying, unpleasant, decaying smell. A heavy, lethargic and negative energy.

Little Robert was standing with his mother by the

kitchen window. He was a beautiful, angelic-looking, little fair-haired child. He cowered and buried his head into his mother's hip and clutched her sweater. Approaching him slowly, I could feel the powerful, unmistakable and familiar energy. This was an energy I had encountered before. I was in the presence of an extremely evil entity. A black, dark, evil energy emanated from him. A black cloud surrounded his aura.

He looked up at me – slowly at first, in total fear – but then I saw his eyes. They turned black and I found myself looking into the face of Satan himself.

The evil malevolence gleaming in his eyes and his manic grin knocked me backwards, almost off my feet, so powerful was he. Still it was he who was frightened of me. I am familiar with the way he retaliates, being the focus of many of his attacks, which have become increasingly stronger since I began to perform exorcisms and even more so since I began to relay the messages of Our Lady.

"How are you doing, Robert?" I asked the child, bending down.

Darting away, he ran and hid under the kitchen table, cowering and huddling into a tiny ball like a terrified little kitten. Meanwhile, the baby was in the pram at the other end of the kitchen.

"I need you to concentrate," I explained to the parents. "You need to understand exactly what I intend to do here. You may hear obscenities from the child. You may hear him divulge private, embarrassing things about each of you. But you must turn a deaf ear," I told them. "Be on your guard at all times. I am going to use holy water to give you a special blessing for protection. Then I need to seal off the kitchen."

I asked Hannah to pick the baby up. Then I blessed the child in the name of Jesus on her forehead, throat, heart and, finally, on her crown. I then blessed her in the Name of the Father. I repeated the ritual with the mother and finally with Brian. During all this time, Robert was as quiet as a mouse. He was still hiding under the table.

Moving quickly now, as soon as I lit the candles I immediately splashed holy water under the table. I could hear the child shifting quickly. There followed a moment of complete silence. The blood-curdling, high-pitched, piercing scream that then followed was deafening. It was the scream of a demon. A sound you'd never want to hear, ever again. The shrillness, which caused the room to vibrate, chilled us to the bone. Trembling with absolute terror now, Brian and Hannah fell back and held tightly onto each other, with the baby pressed between them.

The ceremony started in earnest then with me saying, out loud, the "Hail Mary", the special prayer to the Blessed Mother, the Holy Mother of God, the Virgin. I called then on the archangels, including Michael, Gabriel, Raphael and all the holy angels as well as St John the Baptist and St Joseph.

The sealing process then began, so that I could bring Light into the house. Every corner in the kitchen was splashed with holy water. I splashed the windows and each door until I had, finally, trapped the demon.

After about ten minutes of constant prayer, there was still no sign of him – the Evil One – except for a little whimpering noise. Plucking up the courage, on my instructions, Robert's mother yanked him out from under the table. It took every ounce of energy, because of his frantic kicking and screaming, to finally set him on a chair facing all of us. Hannah held onto him fast. He stared straight ahead for more than five minutes without once blinking his eyes. That's when I heard the first loud knock from a door somewhere.

As the prayers continued, I turned on the music. The beautiful haunting sound of the *Ave Maria* hymn filled every square inch of the room. I sat directly opposite the child, face to face, holding my crucifix. I tried to look back into his staring eyes, where he looked into space in a kind of catatonic state, but it was as if he was staring right through me.

To my relief, I finally felt the room begin to fill with a special light. I sensed Michael the Archangel on my right side. Mesmerised, I saw that Jesus was also present in the room. The love and light from him was palpable and filled me with so much more courage. He stood right behind the child. Visible only from the waist up, I could see his hands were spread out over the child's head, as if in prayer, and I could see his heart clearly beating. It looked exactly as you would see in any image of the Sacred Heart of Jesus.

Crouching now, arms covering his head, Robert let out a long drawn-out moan. A deep guttural sound could be heard as his body began to sway from side to side. Suddenly his head shot up, wrenching his body into an upright confrontational position. His face contorted into an evil grin, he hissed at me, "You f****** c**t! You won't get me!"

"In the name of Jesus Christ, I command you to tell me who you are," I said. This question is always necessary in order to establish if it is Satan himself or one of his followers, and if there is one demon present or many, and so gauge the strength of the possession.

His wide glaring black eyes looked straight into my soul. I felt my chest tighten. Then he squealed at the top of his voice in the highest pitch humanly possible, and spat at me.

Once again I asked him, "In the name of Jesus Christ, I command you to tell me who you are! Is your name Satan? Lucifer? Whose name do you come in?"

He continued to stare at me, again without blinking. Obscenities no child would ever have any knowledge of came tumbling from his little mouth. A litany of vile, disgusting and horrific blasphemies spewed forth. Then it began to change. New multiple voices were coming out, all speaking at once, with such dizzying speed that it seemed as if the room was filled with a loud buzzing noise. The buzzing continued, the sound louder and louder until you felt you had to place your hands over your ears or they would burst. Then the smell came. It was like a bad sewer, but worse. I gagged, just as I heard a second loud knock. This time it seemed to be coming from a window somewhere.

"In the name of Jesus Christ, I command you for the final time to tell me your name!" I cried.

His eyes rolled right into the back of his head so that only the whites showed and I then heard the voice of an adult male. The pitch was so strong it would have knocked me back had I not the protection of the crucifix.

"You know who I am," he hissed. "I'm not afraid of you!"

"Who are you?" I asked again, the crucifix in his face. "Are you here at the command of Satan? Are you one of the fallen angels? Are you Satan himself?"

"No. I'm not the Prince. I'm not one, I am many of his angels," came the reply.

I knew at that point that I was dealing with a number of demon spirits.

Then, when the third knock came, this time from the ceiling, I knew I was close to the breaking point. The three knocks during an exorcism are Satan's way of mocking the Holy Trinity. So loud was the knock this time that the room vibrated.

We were in the final stages now. I raised up the crucifix and commanded in the Name of Jesus Christ that these wicked demons leave this body now. I said this three times. After that, I finally held the cross to the child's forehead. As he writhed in agony, the demon then blew out of him with such force you could feel it, hear it, like a rushing, strong gale-force wind.

Then a quiet, peaceful calm came over the room and everyone in it. I felt, immediately, that Jesus had his hand held protectively over Robert. I was filled with love and joy. I knew Jesus was with us. We were safe.

With that, the child collapsed in a heap on the floor. Hannah gently tapped him on the cheek. He yawned and woke up. His face lit up when he looked at his mother. Then he flung his hands around her neck and sobbed happily in her arms.

Since that time Robert has been a happy, well-behaved child and a joy to his parents.

7

People who Sell their Souls to the Devil

It may surprise you to hear that many people, even in today's world of modern science and technological wonders do, in fact, sell their souls to the Devil. Yes, it's true, and it's more common than you think. Because there has been a resurgence in the practice of satanic masses and an extraordinary interest in the occult, people are now ideally primed to attract the Evil One.

There is another reason. When people lived a more basic, simple life, without access to excessive materialist corruption, they believed in God. Irrespective of the religious path they were on, most people believed, or their parents believed, in God. They believed in love of one another. They strived and did their best to consciously live a good life, to show love and respect to each other. Prayer and a belief in God lightened their mood. People also believed in the Devil and knew the dangers he posed.

Today, while outwardly not admitting to believe in the Evil One, his ways are welcomed with open arms because of the wonderful promises he makes. He, his works and his extraordinary world are seen as completely fascinating and powerfully compelling. So much so that it has spawned a huge number of occult and vampire-type TV programmes, movies and books.

So who really sells their souls to the Devil? Do you think this is just part and parcel of a fantasy? Well, you have to start by looking to where Satan looks first. He targets intelligent, smart, ambitious people – particularly those in positions of power. Political and church leaders are his favourite primary targets. Because music is such a powerful communications tool that appeals to the spirit, this is one area that Satan focuses on. I believe he targets those in the entertainment industry. In order to be successful, rich and powerful, many rock stars, all of whom are prime targets of Satan, can end up signing a pact with him. Many have publicly admitted to signing a pact with the Devil, others have hinted at it publicly and these stories are there for everyone to see and decide for themselves. I believe some may be caught unwittingly. Others know exactly what they are doing. Whatever their reasons, the temptation of success is hard to resist in their mind's eye. And this has been happening for centuries. How many times do you see staring right at you an obscene spectacle of "success" stories, exceptional wealth, celebrity spending sprees and so-called musical talent, which would have been deemed mediocre less than twenty years ago, but is applauded a little too loudly today.

And it doesn't stop there. Some rock stars and rappers can leave clues within their work as part of their badge of Satan. Is this true? Yes. It sounds archaic, medieval perhaps. But if you look closely at the lyrics, for example, in some of the world's most famous bestselling albums, you will find strange mutterings going on. The lyrics, in some, openly admire Satan and boast of the selling of people's souls.

Other outward clues, such as the upside-down cross symbol of Satan, which was designed by satanic cults as a mockery and Jesus chokers are often seen worn around the neck of many rock performers.

Another giveaway sign is the secret hand-sign known as the "El Diablo" sign (not to be confused with the love hand-sign, which is similar), which was a common salute used by one recent world leader, rock artists and wealthy movie stars. Why do they do it? To help followers of Satan to identify their allegiance. Because, you see, even if they are afraid to publicly declare their allegiance with Satan, their arrogance knows no bounds. The urge for yet more adoration kicks in to encourage others to admire their "leap into power". It's hard to resist. A risky gesture, yes, but a calculated risk to openly boast that they, too, have forged a pact with the Devil.

As for the sceptics – better think again. Satan's

other targets are today's eminent modern intellectual establishment. And this to me is the most dangerous form of infestation of all because it will have an impact on our democracy and future freedom.

Scientists, economists, psychiatrists, doctors, politicians, world leaders, judges – very few escape his clutches. Satan is instantly attracted to intelligent people. Intelligent and cunning as he is, he feels right at home in any refined intellectual comfort zone. Any seemingly smart, logical arguments presented, "proving" that God is a figment of our imagination, excite and delight him. Books that proclaim the "idolatry" they associate with a belief in the spirit world, God, Heaven and Hell, are all works of Satan. He has been the inspiration behind them. Disguised behind a new modern "philosophical thinking", these books set out to do just one thing: deny that God exists. And they succeed. It's then that Satan is set loose, to cause total fear, havoc, confusion and hatred by infesting God's children through his evil lies.

Just like in the Garden of Eden in the Book of Genesis, the Devil, through his lies, convinces people to eat of the forbidden fruit. When people sell their soul to Satan, he promises wonderful gifts – power on this Earth, amazing success, health, happiness and incredible wealth. He'll tell you that you can reach the dizziest heights of success. Materially, you'll never want for more. You'll never feel the need to turn back. In return for your soul, he tells the lie.

Global Conspiracies

I believe Satan is active in large corporate but secret organisations (often disguised as conservative right-wing Christian and Catholic movements). Hiding behind the "establishment" they operate in such secrecy that even the lower echelons of their organisations are not aware of what is really going on. Without mentioning these organisations by name, they represent a powerful Global feudal system, reminiscent of the Middle Ages. They do their work behind closed doors and through powerful secret societies made up of some of the world's most powerful leaders. All of this will culminate in Satan's plans for leading a world power.

Satanic culture also permeates influential, very secret, so-called religious-based institutions, including a number of conservative Christian organisations. Most of these secret societies are cloaked under the guise of Christianity when, in fact, they are anything but Christian. The stark reality is that the "God" they worship is completely different to that of mainstream Christian belief. They actually refer to the Christian God as an "inferior god". So effective are they that they have managed to weave a powerful web of deceit around their activities. Even those who consider themselves to be intelligent are conditioned into believing they don't exist.

The symbols used in their practices are very similar to those used in occult practices. And just as occultists believe that once a symbol is created, it acquires its own power, the symbols used by these so-called Christian societies go so far as to glorify the sex act just as you expect an occult group to do.

Even more alarming is the probable truth of the view that a number of leading politicians and renowned and esteemed professionals covering every single area of life – doctors, sports people, actors, military and clergy – are secret members. I must point out and make it absolutely clear, however, that many well-meaning high-standing individuals join these organisations in absolute good faith. I know that they are completely genuine and have only the best of intentions. Unfortunately, they are being deceived. Because it's only in the very highest tiers within these organisations that satanic practices really come into their own. That's where the real power lies.

So what? What harm are they doing? The answer is simple. They're dangerous because they have an agenda. It's an agenda that has a bearing on all of us in the world. They also pose a serious threat to world stability because of the control they have. Globalisation is a frightening concept for this very reason. Remember, it has been prophesied in the Bible, in the Book of Revelation, that Satan will hide within such organisations.

People need to be on their guard against any religious teaching that does not conform to the teachings of the Bible. When it doesn't, you can assume that its preachers are what is constantly referred to in the Bible as "false prophets". As Christ himself warned,

"*Beware of false prophets, who come to you in sheep's clothing but inwardly are ravening wolves.*"

For those believers in God who are preparing for the Second Coming, they must never lose sight of the fact that the biggest threat facing all of us comes from Satan, the Evil One. He will work discreetly, silently, behind the scenes. Much as I hate to say it, he will take position at the heart of a major new political or religious world order of some kind.

In the Bible, you can see where Satan boasted, "*I will be like the Most High*". Unfortunately, he will also sit in the temple of God and, as we learn in the Book of Revelation, "*All that dwell upon the Earth shall worship him*". He has already started and begins by targeting the most influential sectors of society, especially the clergy, who are always his number one target. Sadly, he has targeted the Catholic Church and the numerous cases of child abuse are testament to this.

Earth is already going through a huge and unpleasant upheaval, with great changes sweeping the world, almost on a weekly basis. Christians face challenges every single day, challenges that come in every shape and size. At every conceivable level, they present themselves, and most are so subtle and "innocent" that many people find it hard to believe.

As I already said, there has been a surging new interest in the occult, which is seen and published in a "novelty" way through films, magazines and books. Even children have been targeted by the promotion of an avid interest in sorcery through books and games. The sad thing is that many people do not believe that any of this is related to Satan or Christian religions, because they simply are not aware of the truth behind the physical realm.

Anything that diverts attention away from spiritual values is the first thing to watch out for. We have all been there. You know when you are being challenged to take part in something – a scheme, a task or a certain direction – that you know is inherently wrong, against your moral standards.

Lobby groups and other organisations set up to appeal to people to pursue pleasure, pride and power are a giveaway sign. Those who encourage permissiveness, damaging moral and ethical values, are working in my view from the side of Darkness.

The Woman Who Sold her Soul to Satan

My third exorcism involved a woman I'll refer to as "Bernie" who turned her back on God and promised Satan allegiance if he would rescue her from poverty. He did. But that's when her real problems began.

I was standing at my local bus stop at eleven o'clock one Friday night when my mobile phone rang. I had no sooner answered it when I heard the most incredible sounds coming from the other end. I could hear a loud squealing, an ear-piercing squeaky little voice first; then an unmerciful deep guttural roar. "You won't f****** save me, you f****** c**t! Come near me and I'll f****** kill you!" Then silence. Gone.

I was shocked. Did I really hear all that? I looked at the phone. No record of any call showed up. No number.

Seconds later, the mobile rang again. It was a young man I will call "Cormac", who had tried to convince me, weeks earlier, that his mother was possessed by the Devil. I had told him and his father "Tom" to take her to see a priest. There had been no word from them since then, until now.

"Help us, Joe," he whispered. "Did you hear that? That was her – she found the number you gave me and rang you. Did you hear her voice? It's not human –" He never got to finish. I could hear a struggle as the phone was whipped from him, and a man's scream where she had obviously physically hurt him.

Then the terrible voice was back on again.

"Listen here you f****** c**t. What did I tell you? Stay away from me or I'll kill you!" the thing roared at me. Suddenly, unexpectedly, the voice switched tone and in an almost girly voice began speaking rapidly in Spanish!

Then there was a silence.

"Cormac! Cormac!" I called, hoping he was still on the line.

"Yes, just about." He sounded breathless. "She really hurt me just now. She's so strong – we're trying to keep her pinned to the bed."

"What's happening? Who's with you?" I asked.

"My dad. We've put her into bed. She's attacking us – throwing things at us. She just has to look at the things to move them!" he gasped. I could hear the struggle in the background and the roars of his mother. I could feel his terror.

"Why didn't you call the priest like I told you?" I asked him.

"I did," he told me. "We brought her to see him tonight. But the poor man was terrified. He said he didn't know how to do an exorcism. He told us to go home and pray. We scared the life out of him. I don't blame him. If you saw the state of her, you'd run a mile. We just took her home to her bed. It's safer. Joe, please help us."

How could I say no? I knew, though, that under no circumstances was I going to handle this one on my own! The thing is, most exorcisms are mild and mainly boring affairs. All that's involved is a prayer ceremony, consecration and blessing. Very few are dramatic. The exception, of course, is what is known as real diabolic possession – the most serious form of demonic activity. I had no doubt: Cormac's mother, Bernie, fell into this category. It wasn't until much later that I found out that we were also dealing with what's called a diabolic subjugation. In simple language, this means a voluntary pact with the Evil One, where the possessed has willingly, and knowingly, submitted to his temptations. Combine the two, and you've got the most potent and dangerous cocktail of all. I had no idea when I set out for their house that night that we were about to face the strongest dual combination of satanic possession imaginable.

I took Seán, my son, with me. Seán is psychically gifted and has been since the day he was born. Like me, he can see the spirits of people who have passed from this life. He is a good young man, has a deep faith and a belief in his maker. He is one with God and lives "in the Light". He, too, has an affiliation with Michael the Archangel and feels him at his side daily. A young man, still in college, he is not the type who shouts publicly about his gift. He's the last person who would want to bring unnecessary attention to himself. But Seán also has the power to stand up to Satan.

He has seen the Evil One at work many times, especially in homes which are infested. Like me, he has no fear of the Prince of Darkness, Satan. Because of his deep faith, which is unwavering in its intensity, he is a powerful adversary of the Evil One. He is one with God. He is fearless confronting Satan. I have seen him in action and he impresses me. I trust him. And wasn't I glad I took him with me that night!

When we reached the house we found the door opened at a push. Going in, we stopped in amazement as the freezing temperature hit us. Just the beginning, I thought. We could hear raised voices and screams upstairs. We cautiously went up.

We had only just reached the top when we heard

what can only be described as the roar of a lion. Deep, low, extremely loud, it was directed at me: "I *warned* you to stay away, Joe Coleman!" the voice screamed at us from behind a door.

Pausing, Seán and I blessed ourselves with holy water, sprinkling it on us and on the door itself. Holding my large crucifix up in front of me, I walked slowly into the bedroom, Seán behind me. We had just entered the room from hell.

The stench assailed our nostrils forcibly as soon as we closed the door. The smell of rotting, decaying flesh and human excrement was so strong that we gagged. We couldn't stop ourselves. Grabbing tissues out of our pockets, we covered our noses. We turned around and took in slowly, in disbelief, the incredible scene in front of us.

Flanked on each side by her husband Tom and son Cormac, the woman, Bernie, was lying flat on the bed. She looked filthy, like a wounded wild animal – hair wild, uncombed and matted, arms and legs bruised, with dry scabs everywhere. Her nightgown was badly stained with dried vomit, spots of blood and urine. We couldn't see her face. It was turned away from us, facing into the wall – on purpose, I thought. No surprise there. Her son was doing his level best to hold her feet down while her poor unfortunate husband was trying to keep her upper body down in the bed. She kept trying to sit up. The more she tried, the more they kept pinning her down.

While Seán turned on the music of the *Ave Maria* track, I began sprinkling holy water on every surface in the room – into each corner, on the bed, the walls, the window and the inner side of the door. As soon as the room was consecrated, I made the Sign of the Cross, using holy water, on her husband and son.

Bernie turned slowly and slyly to face me, her eyes averted downwards; she would not look me in the face. Instead, she let out a stream of obscenities as soon as Seán and I began praying. Growling like a dog, she bared her teeth, pulled her lips back and laughed at me. To my disgust, I saw that her teeth were pointed, larger than human teeth and tainted a dirty yellow. Howling with laughter, she began to taunt me. "I know all about you, Joe Coleman! I know your soul – your sins! You can't fool me. You'll never get me." As soon as I sprinkled the holy water on her – it splashed her forehead – she let out a terrifying roar of pure pain. To everyone's horror, it burned her and we could see the steam coming from her.

We continued our prayers. Then I demanded to know who she was. No response, just moaning, groaning, writhing in the bed. She tried to pull herself up in the bed again.

"Oh Joe, you are hurting me, please stop," she pleaded, this time in a calm, lady-like voice.

I continued, "I command you in the name of Jesus Christ to tell me who you are!" I splashed more holy water.

Then slowly, her chest seemed to swell and blow up like a balloon. Eyes downwards, still unable to look at me, she shook off her husband and son with inhuman strength, pulled herself up and spat at me. I repeated the command again. No answer.

Then her body lifted slowly, stiff as a poker, until it was lying flat about one foot above the bed.

This isn't happening, I thought. *It can't be.*

I decided to move to her left side and give her son a break. No sooner had I done this than she began to scream again. Then she began to moan more softly. As we prayed more intensely now, the woman began to calm down. The power of the *Ave Maria* music was working because she began sinking back into the bed.

"Bernie," I asked her, "are you feeling okay? A little better?"

"Oh, yes," she replied. "Yes, much better. Thanks so much."

"That's good. Bernie, we are here to help you. Prayer will drive the demon away, but you have to work with us. Do you understand?"

"Yes, Joe," she replied. "Can you let me hold your cross?" She was indicating the cross around my neck.

I took it off and handed it to her gently. She took it – and then threw it with an almighty powerful force at Seán, cackling at the top of her voice.

The most extraordinary thing happened just then. The cross stopped suddenly in mid-air in front of Seán's face, then turned around and hurled itself into the concrete wall, where it became firmly embedded. *Impossible*, I thought.

This was followed by horrible sickening laughter from the depths of evil. The woman squealed with delight, "You stupid f*****! Do you think I'm that stupid?"

The music continued. I prayed over her, my large crucifix in front of her face.

"Joe, you're hurting me so badly. Turn that music off."

"I command you in the name of God to reveal your name!" I continued, still praying with every ounce of strength in me.

Then she turned black, doleful eyes at me with a look of pure affection. Blinking, I looked down at her.

"Joe, my darling, it's me," she said in a sweet, pleading voice.

Swallowing hard, with tears stinging my eyes, I realised it was the voice of someone very close to me who had passed some years before.

"Please don't hurt me any more, Joe," the voice begged me.

I felt I was about to cry and struggled to keep the tears at bay.

"I command, in the name of Jesus Christ, that you reveal yourself!" I bent over the bed with the crucifix in front of me and the Bible in my hand.

Vicious, evil eyes then locked with mine and the inhuman, almost baritone voice, spat at me, "I am

Satan, the Prince of Darkness. You will never overpower me!"

Holding the crucifix high in front of me, I said, "I work in the name of Jesus Christ. I will overpower you. I command you now to leave this woman's body. I will continue to burn you with this Holy Water until you leave."

I continued to sprinkle holy water on her. Every time I did, it was like throwing water on a hot pan filled with hot oil. Her skin sizzled each time, the burning steam wafting in the air.

Cormac cried uncontrollably. He couldn't bear to watch this thing that his mother had become. I thought he was going to faint and told him to leave the room.

"No, Joe, I am not going until this bastard has left her!" he cried.

I was off guard and she suddenly raised her hand and tried to grab my bottle of holy water, but she missed. I felt her claws dig into me as she tore the buttons off my shirt. One by one they snapped off.

Just then, as if nothing had been happening, she began to chat amicably. "How are you, Joe? You can go now – I'm okay now!"

I began to coax her gently as I prayed over her. When I felt the time was right, I placed a picture of the Holy Spirit in the form of a dove on her chest. She darted up so fast in the bed that I was thrown back. She grabbed the picture, which was made of thick cardboard, and started chewing it into a ball in her mouth. She kept chewing and munching, her face contorted in the most grotesque manner as she tried to swallow it. I had to turn away; I found it so hard to look at her. Suddenly, she turned her head and spat it out at Seán. Once again an extraordinary thing happened. The ball of cardboard came within an inch of Seán's face, stopped and plopped right down onto the bed.

Levitating once again, she twisted and thrashed as the men now tried unsuccessfully to keep her pinned down. Under his breath, Seán then quietly said the special prayer to St Michael the Archangel, calling on him to use his sword to cut the ties from the demon.

"Oh Seán, please, you are hurting my legs!" she screamed as her body stiffened in pure agony. To our utter astonishment, we could see deep scars – no blood, but new deep welt-like sores – appearing one by one. We knew then that it was Michael the Archangel at work. All this happened while we held onto her legs and upper body, never once loosening our grip.

Again I shouted the command for Satan to leave the woman's body. Turning her head slowly, she looked at me – black and shark-like, right into my soul. With an evil grin – like that of a monster – her teeth seemed to get bigger and uglier. Her teeth had changed beyond all human resemblance. I must admit, it was very frightening. Her mouth was snarling now like a wild dog and I could see her tongue. It was a big red "dog-like" tongue, hanging out, panting.

We started gagging again, as the smell was getting worse. It was really sickening now. Satan always tries to infest your aura. This is one of the ways he tries to do it.

I continued my prayers over her, my commands getting stronger and stronger. She suddenly grabbed my arm and forced me down to confront her close up, right up to her stinking face. Then she smiled in the most grotesque way as she seemed to be trying to squeeze something in her hand. I felt suddenly tremendous pain. My heart was being squeezed. It was as if she had taken it in her powerful paws and begun to crush it slowly, with tremendous strength. I could feel my insides being twisted. The pain was excruciating. I thought I was having a heart attack. I fell backwards.

Seán caught me. "Dad, take a break. Go on, sit down. But please don't give up. You can't give up."

"Okay, son, let me sit down for a while; you keep on with the prayers."

I was worn out by now, drained of all energy and filled with a dreadful sense of disappointment. I felt I wasn't getting anywhere.

"This is not working," I said to Seán.

"Dad, you can't give up! We're nearly there! We can't!" Seán pleaded. He could see the effect it was all having on me.

Of course I had no intention of stopping. This was my duty. It had to be done, no matter how long it was going to take.

"Don't let the bastard win!" said Seán. "He wants to convince you to believe that he will kill you. He's trying to frighten you."

The speaking in tongues continued. She babbled in so many languages and in so many voices, but Spanish was the one that seemed to be most constant.

Looking at her now from the chair, I couldn't help but notice the huge number of other, older cuts all over her body.

"She has been mutilating herself," said Cormac. "She's been at this for over a month now. She uses knives, scissors, nails even, anything she can get her hands on."

We continued praying constantly, the *Ave Maria* blaring from the corner of the room. On and on we went. Then objects – ornaments, pictures – began to fly everywhere before crashing against the wall.

Suddenly pandemonium broke out. Her head shot back. She began to bang her head with tremendous force off the wall. I really began to worry for her. Back and back again; I thought she would smash her skull in. The screams, the obscenities, were coming out now with such an intensity that I knew we were about to witness another episode of some kind.

"Bernie!" her husband called. "Bernie, we love you, please let him loose!"

"Oh Tom, I'm so scared. Hold me!"

As he leaned over to take her close, she grabbed him by the arm and sank her sharp animal teeth into his skin, taking a huge piece of flesh, the size of a golf ball, into her mouth. She chewed on it for a bit, then swallowed it whole, grinning at us the entire time. Tom screamed in pain and terror, blood splashing everywhere as he ran downstairs to call for an ambulance.

"Joe," she called me then, "I know everything about you! I know your future. You have no power over me. You can't touch me."

Weary by now, but determined to fight this, I began to pray even more in earnest now, this time to Our Blessed Mother. I started the Rosary while a weary Seán once again splashed her with holy water.

After four hours we finally broke the spell. Screaming obscenities still, but weaker this time, she eventually broke down.

I asked her how she was feeling. In a weak, barely audible voice, she said she felt better. Then she broke down and cried. I blew the Holy Spirit into her. I told her to renounce Satan now – which she did, for the first time. I told her Jesus was back in her soul and she was never to allow the Evil One in again.

Then a loud whooshing sound, like the rush of a wind, could be heard. At last! It was the Evil One, the vile Prince of Darkness, departing her poor wretched body. So it was that we finally won her soul back.

We left that house in the early hours of the

morning, more than four hours after we had arrived. Our work was over.

While I hope now that I don't have to handle too many exorcisms, I realise that I have a duty. I fully understand that by accepting this gift, I have become marked for life and will be a constant target of the Evil One to the day I die. But he will never defeat me.

How to Protect Ourselves from Satan

So how do we protect ourselves from Satan? Our Lady has told me that the first thing we must do, when we are feeling stressed or vulnerable, is to make a special request to her. We must ask her to place her "sacred mantle" around us and our families. She cannot just come and do this; you must ask her. As she cannot interfere with our own free will, it's important to ask. The same applies to Jesus: ask in order to receive.

There are a number of ways in which we can protect ourselves, starting with prayer:

- *Prayer:* This is one of the most powerful weapons against the Deceiver. By praying, you will draw God's power around you.
- *Holy Water*: You should always have blessed holy water in your house, your office or wherever you work.

- *Rosary Beads:* If you are Catholic, try to carry a set of rosary beads blessed by a priest with you wherever you go.

- *Brown Scapular:* Offered by Our Lord and Our Lady, this Holy Scapular helps to lead us through the terrible times when the world will face the holy wrath of God. Our Lord and His Holy Mother Our Lady manifest themselves in the person who wears it. It will help in any torment. Try to get hold of a Holy Scapular, available from the Carmelite Order.

- *Benedictine Cross*: One of the most powerful antidotes against Satan; try to get one that is blessed by a priest and wear it as often as possible.

- *Symbols:* While you don't have to have symbols, they are useful in helping to remind you of God and all his saints and as a help during prayer. These can be statues, pictures, medals etc.

- *White Light:* You can also protect yourself by calling in your angels. Ask them to surround your body with pure white light. That way, your aura is protected. When you ask your angels to send you this gift of a beautiful white light, it represents the higher source of energy that comes from God, like a protective shield. Anyone that follows Satan and his evil ways will see and feel this light from you and they will know, instantly, that you are being protected.

- There is one simple prayer that offers one of the most powerful protections of all, and that you should say every morning before you start your day: *"I am one with God; there is no separation."*
- Catholics should make sure they receive Confession at least once a month, and receive the Holy Eucharist at least once a week.
- You must ask Our Lord for special graces for protection. If you are working in the area of healing, for example, you must ensure you dedicate your space to God every single day. For it brings the Light, the healing energy and the good angels.
- The final and most important secret of all is not just carrying but saying the Holy Rosary. By saying the Rosary once a day, you will not only protect yourself and your family, but you will help them enter the Kingdom of Heaven on the final day of judgment.

Taking action to protect ourselves leaves us free to live the good, peaceful and contented life we need to live in order to please God. It means also that we can avoid exposing ourselves and our families, as well as close personal friends, from being sucked into the cunning schemes of Satan. If you are unfortunate enough to be snared by the Evil One, it is very difficult to free yourself from him. As I said before, his biggest talent is to convince people he doesn't exist, so it is nearly impossible to know if and when you have been "infected".

8

The Gift of Physical Healing

I realised I had developed the gift of physical healing when in 2007 I met a woman with terminal cancer who was beyond help medically, with only weeks to live. Yet her spirit, her belief in God the Father, his Son Jesus and the Holy Spirit was inspiring. As soon as I prayed over her in my little healing room and asked her to join me in prayer, I found myself automatically placing my right hand on her head, without really understanding why. It just seemed the right thing to do. Immediately I could feel pins and needles, and a strong vibration shot through my right hand. Then I felt a burning sensation. My hand was so hot it felt like it was on fire.

That was the first time that this had ever happened to me and, although it was a shock and I found it overwhelming, it was a beautiful feeling. I couldn't believe it. I was shaking with a mixture of shock, joy and complete amazement. Although this was new to me I knew immediately, there and then, that I had been given this grace by God for a reason. It was God working through me, this time as a physical healing channel.

A month later, the same woman, who had been suffering from terminal breast cancer, with no hope at all, called to tell me that a scan had just revealed she was cured. No traces of the cancer could be found anywhere. She described it as a miracle. She was indeed cured and by the hand of Jesus.

Another case was that of a young mother who was diagnosed with leukaemia. She had been through every kind of chemo treatment and was given very little time to live – a matter of days only – by the time I saw her in hospital. She was surrounded by her family and they had all come to terms with the fact that she would die, including the woman herself. I prayed over her for a full hour, healing her with the power of the Holy Spirit. Even though the husband had been sceptical, the rest of the family had hope. Three weeks later, to the astonishment of the doctors, she left the hospital fully recovered. It was a miracle.

The gift of healing was, and still is to this day, a deeply humbling experience and one for which I am eternally grateful to God. I am touched and honoured that He uses me as a channel. Yet I know I am not the only one He has chosen. I believe He has given this same gift to thousands of his followers on this Earth for a reason. Just as I am sure that this healing gift has been divinely inspired, I now completely understand what the healings represent and why I was given this gift in the first place.

I believe Jesus is trying to give those who are healed a "message". When Jesus performed healings during His time on Earth, it was done with one purpose in mind. He wanted to show people His love, but He also wanted to encourage them, through the healing process, to say "yes" to him. Yes, to acknowledge the deep unconditional love He has for all of his children. Yes, to say that we do believe and, yes, to say we will follow His teachings. And yes, to follow Him thereafter with prayer and devotion.

Soon after the first cures became public knowledge, I started to get phone calls and letters from people who were sick, stressed or emotionally drained, asking for faith-healing. People were always at my door and life became hectic. It didn't matter what the problem was, I would try to help them. I never refused a healing though I was obliged to take some weekends off to recover my energy. It was time-consuming and exhausting. I was doing all of this voluntarily although I did accept donations to cover my costs.

Before beginning a healing, I would always light a candle and say a prayer. During any healing session, whether it was for a spiritual cleansing only or for a physical healing, as soon as I started the prayer, the tingling and heat sensation in my right hand started. I noticed that I found my hand focusing on the head and heart if they were emotionally upset and on the exact part of the body where disease resided if they were ill. I always began with the spiritual healing, which can take some time, and it always involved prayer.

I would become concerned when, sometimes, the person who had come for the healing would say, "But Joe, I just wanted to be cured from the disease. I am not religious. I'm not really interested in the spiritual side of things." I would always reply, "Inner spiritual healing is important and has to come first." Real permanent physical healing can only take place when it accompanies healing of the spirit. I also, of course, secretly suspect that many health problems are rooted in and connected to a deep unhappiness of the soul. These people are empty inside. They are simply surviving in what they perceive to be a meaningless life, and it's usually because their spirit is dead.

When people hear about a "miracle cure" they get very excited and immediately associate the cure with just the healing of the physical body. Not everyone is cured, though. I don't know why. And because it is Jesus who is working through me during my healing, I cannot speak for Him. I believe, though, that in any healing, special graces will be given to that person, whether or not physical healing results.

So when a person today asks me to "cure" them, the first thing I do is to pray with them. I ask them first of all to look into their hearts and review their life. I tell them to look at the areas in their lives that cause them deep unhappiness and uneasiness. I then ask them to be honest with themselves for a moment. I give them time. It is important that they are relaxed and quiet. In some cases, they may have no faith, no belief of any kind. I explain to them that they need to start searching into their souls and to honestly evaluate their lives – how they live, how they treat others and themselves, including how they damage their own bodies. I tell them they must ask God to help them "wipe the slate clean". Above all, they must ask for God's forgiveness for any wrongdoing. It's important to realise that when Jesus performed healings during his lifetime, He always said to those people who came to him, *"Your sins are forgiven."* It was only then that He healed them physically.

When a person truly opens up with their heart, they will be spiritually healed and, if they are physically sick, they may be cured. But this is entirely at God's will. While we can ask God for anything and He will listen and do His best to grant the request, He cannot be manipulated into doing what you want Him to do. The final decision is His. He doesn't "jump to attention" and never changes just to suit us. We must change to suit Him. It's that simple. Everything is according to His will.

My first prayer, after lighting the candle, would be to dedicate the space to God Most High, the Holy Spirit. I would ask for love, light and healing energy as well as protection for the person in question. Then I would say the following prayer:

"God, my hands are Your hands. I give thanks for them. I ask for Your guidance in using them to bless others. Fill my hands with Your love and use them to bring comfort when there is pain, encouragement where there is despair. Guide my hands and fill them with Your strength so that I may help the ones who need to be uplifted. Your work in my hands is a true labour of love and I am grateful for every opportunity to bring peace and joy to others. Bless my hands and make them an instrument of Your peace. Empower my hands with the skill they need to accomplish Your almighty work."

I then call on my angels, including Michael the Archangel. He always stands and protects me during the healing so that I cannot be attacked by the Evil One. Because when you are doing healing with God's blessing you can be "attacked" by Satan and if he does you won't be able to pray properly and he mixes you up.

Some spiritual healers claim that they can perform healing with the natural spirit energies that exist within the universe. That's okay. But I will always ask the question, "Who made the universe?" The answer is obvious.

Those who were cured often came back and told me that it was through the healing they experienced through me that they had, at last, found a new spiritual faith and a belief in God again. Their renewed faith gave them a new meaning for life. They felt love again in their lives and a deeper connection to people. Many reported feeling more patient with other people and a greater willingness to treat other people more kindly. I now know that Jesus sometimes heals the physically disabled or terminally ill to do just that, to renew their spiritual faith.

Something else that people may not realise is that when a person is miraculously cured by God from, say, a terminal illness, this may not be the end of it! These people are usually asked to "carry His cross" in return. This may not happen in the immediate aftermath of the cure, but much later. I have seen and heard of this happening time and time again. It could be that the person in question may feel a sudden "pull" towards prayer at a later stage. Or they may feel drawn into helping the sick or disabled on a voluntary basis. One way or the other they will, at some stage, feel obliged to give back what they have received in God's name. They will know instinctively the time they are called.

Learning How to Pray Again

In response to this wonderful healing ministry given to me, I became even closer to God the Eternal Father, his son Jesus Christ and the Holy Spirit, and continued with my very special devotion to Our Blessed Mother, the Virgin Mary. On the practical side, I had to learn how to pray, as I needed to know how to say prayers out loud during a healing. Not having been a practising Catholic for many years, I had forgotten many of the prayers I learned in school. In fact, I have to admit that I did not know the words of the familiar prayers that most Catholics use. It pains me to admit that I could not, for the life of me, recite a full version of the Lord's Prayer from beginning to end without stumbling. Nor could I say the Rosary in its entirety – I couldn't remember all the Mysteries, for example, nor could I say the "Hail, Holy Queen" prayer at the end. That didn't stop me from praying in my own way. However, I realise now how powerful prayer is. Many people actually don't realise it. But unless you ask God for something, he doesn't give it to you. You cannot receive what you don't ask for.

Prayer is also a very important tool to ward off Satan and his influence in your life.

I had never read the Bible, although as a child in school we were taught the Catechism. Catholics in Ireland are not familiar with the Bible as it is not really taught, with the exception of extracts, in schools. I find this very strange; I just can't understand it. It is only through reading the scriptures that we can fully grasp the teachings of Jesus Christ. And in today's world, where moral values are being swept away and little regard is paid to religion, we all need healing of some kind. I now firmly believe that the full truth of life is contained in the Bible. We can only learn more about Jesus, His teachings and His plans for humanity, in the Bible. He has left us such a wonderful gift. So to understand why we are here, we need to read the Bible.

With the sudden surge of interest the world over in spiritualism at a time of desperate world turmoil, I firmly believe that Jesus is now working closer than ever through ordinary lay people to bring attention to His teachings. It is only through lay people that other people are likely to respond, as they won't feel they are being "preached at". Because of the huge desire for instant gratification, fewer people than ever respond to organised religious representatives of any kind.

I am convinced that God is now actively using lay followers more than before to communicate His messages on this Earth. As He continues to try to get our attention, I think He has been deliberately leaving signs, including the increasing presence of angels in the world, to prompt people to sit up and take note. He needs our help. I believe that He is gathering all His believers in readiness for any redemption plans that lie ahead. He will always work through His followers to communicate His teachings.

The Marian Apparitions

2007–2009

9

Apparition in Kerrytown 2007

I saw my first Apparition of Our Blessed Mother in 2007 – that is, the first since I was a child. In May of that year I was visiting Donegal with friends in Ardara. When I was travelling back to Carrickfinn airport, one of my friends brought me to "The Rock", as it is known, where the grotto of Our Lady is situated in Kerrytown, three miles from Burtonport in West Donegal, a place I had never before heard about. There had been a series of apparitions reported there since 1939 when two teenage girls, aged 19 and 14 years, first claimed to have seen Our Lady on the evening of January 11th 1939 in front of a large granite rock located close to their back garden where the family cottage was situated. They ran immediately back to the cottage and told their family that they had seen a beautiful woman standing on top of the rock that looked like an image of Our Lady.

The image, they claimed, had a radiating light and

was dazzling. She called out to her family and they, along with some neighbours, all went outside to see what was happening. Nine people in total witnessed the event where they said they could feel a very strange presence. But their account of what had happened was dismissed as nonsense by the parish priest. However, eventually, the same priest decided to pay a visit and then claimed to witness the apparition himself and confirmed this in writing.

I had no sooner approached the grotto and knelt down to pray the Rosary when I heard Our Lady speak to me. She whispered to me, *"Joe, my dear child, come back and visit me here on the thirteenth of September. Then I will give you a special message."*

September 12th I returned to The Rock at Kerrytown as Our Lady had requested, and on September 13th she appeared to me there.

So shocked was I, and fearing that people would not believe me, I wrote a letter and gave copies of it to the people in Kerrytown. Before my visit to The Rock I had held a healing session in nearby Dungloe for a group of fifteen people who had heard about me and asked me to see them. It was to these people as well as the local priests I gave the letter.

The letter was as follows:

I, Joe Coleman of the above address, came to Donegal with my friend, Collette Lumdsum and others, on Wednesday 12th September 2007. We took a flight from Dublin to Donegal Airport. We stayed at Bunbeg. On Thursday 13th September 2007 at three o'clock in the afternoon, we were at The Rock in Kerrytown, praying the Rosary. There were about fifty people there, men, women and children. We had got a lift from my pal James Boyle. I stood in front of the statue of Mother Mary. Colette Lumdsum stood on my left side. Most of the other people were in the shelter, or at the side of it. During the first ten minutes I noticed the face of Mary change to her Son Jesus. It then changed to Padre Pio, then back to Jesus, and then back to Mary. I had heard Mary before some months earlier in the summer. She was very beautiful when she appeared to me this time at The Rock. She was crying tears of great sadness for the children of Ireland. She asked me to tell all the people that had come to The Rock that everybody would receive a cure on this day at The Rock. I got very emotional and the tears started to flow down my face. It was a feeling of great joy, great love, unconditional love that came from Mary as she shone her beautiful light out among the crowd. She was crying. She said she was very sad that our young people are not saying the Rosary. She wants all our people to pray and go back to her beloved Son Jesus and come to Him at Mass. She said that there are great changes coming to the Earth and we must pray and ask for guidance and help on our earthly journey. I asked Mary what prayers must we pray. She said, "Pray Our Father, Hail Mary, O Angel of God. You must pray every day. Pray to Padre Pio. He will help you with your prayers." She said she is the Mother of Jesus and she loves all of us very much. She told me I am very special to her, and that she hears my prayers every day. Mother Mary looked very young and pretty, about thirty-five years old. She had a crown of roses on her head. She wore a white gown, no sleeves. She was barefoot with flowers on her feet that were golden daisies. She will come back again. She will tell me when. I had a beautiful day at The Rock. I talk with Mary every day.

Medjugorje

I began to receive messages from Our Lady in 2008 which at first I could not understand. One Tuesday evening, just as I had lit a candle to say my daily Rosary in my little prayer room, I felt a heat around me and I immediately felt her presence.

Then I heard her say, *"Joe, your faith is getting stronger, but I want you to listen now. I need you to carry my cross and spread my message. You have work to do now, Joe. I want you to take Keith to Medjugorje."*

"Why, Mother?" I asked her.

"You both need to be enlightened with the truth and you both need to see me in the most powerful way – a way in which you have never seen me before. Then you will understand why. You will see. I will make known there what it is I want you to do."

The late Keith Henderson was a fellow visionary who had been attending spiritual healing sessions in my prayer room. These sessions, requested by him, were to instil in him a stronger faith and to help him develop a deeper closeness to God. So I borrowed money from the local Credit Union and both of us went to Medjugorje for Easter in April 2009. It was an experience neither of us would ever forget.

As Catholics the world over know, Medjugorje is a town in what used to be Yugoslavia (now Bosnia and Herzegovina) where on June 24th 1981 the Blessed Virgin appeared to six children. She has appeared every day since and Medjugorje has become one of the most popular Catholic places of pilgrimage in the world. Our Lady gives messages on the twenty-fifth of every month to one of the visionaries and on the second of the month to another. Also, people have reported phenomena such as the sun spinning in the sky and figures such as hearts and crosses around the sun. Medjugorje is not officially recognised by the Church but in March 2010 the Pope finally announced the setting up of a commission to investigate it.

Keith and I stayed in a local apartment organised by a travel agency in Dublin, located about four hundreds yards from the main church. Arriving at eight in the evening we booked in and then set out for Apparition Hill by taxi. We got out at the area at the bottom known as the Blue Cross area and then we decided, on impulse, to climb Apparition Hill. I didn't want to go up because it was twilight and I would have preferred to wait until the following day. But Keith was adamant that we go up. I finally gave in. He told me to take my time and follow him.

When I began the slow ascent I was walking awkwardly due to my disability. But then my energy seemed to change. The strange thing was that, despite the pain which I still felt, I found myself climbing without effort and with great strides up the mountain. It took fifteen minutes.

When we reached the top, there was a little moonlight. Not much but enough so that I could clearly see the statue of Our Lady with its railing around it. There were other pilgrims around.

Keith immediately knelt down in front of it with his hands joined in prayer in front of his face. His head was tilted backwards.

I called to him a number of times. "Keith, are you okay?"

No reply. I knew instinctively then that he was in channel with Our Lady.

I noticed that there were three women in a group close by and I could see that they were staring at him. I managed to scramble over the boulders until I stood right behind him. I could see him shaking. As I leaned over to look into his face I noticed the tears rolling down it. He didn't see me. He was in a trance. I knelt down with great difficulty because of the sharp stones and said a decade of the Rosary. It was then that Keith began to join me and say the Rosary out loud with me. When we had finished he looked at me and said: "I saw her crying, Joe." He then broke down again and we stayed there for another fifteen minutes. While I felt the presence of Our Lady throughout the entire time, I didn't see her.

We headed back down the mountain after that, talking non-stop about what had happened. We made our way back to the village and had an early night. The following day we had breakfast and looked around the shops before we went into the local church. During our visit and after a number of private prayers, Keith turned to me and told me he had just seen Our Lady again as well as many angels. He was full of joy.

"Joe," he said suddenly, "I have something to tell you. It wasn't your physical strength that got you up that mountain, it was your faith."

Then on Good Friday we decided to go back up Apparition Hill but, this time, it would be during the day. At noon we got a taxi back to the Hill. Then, with the help of two walking sticks we had bought locally (everyone uses them on the climb up the hill), up we climbed. As soon as we reached the top Keith made his way over to the statute of Our Lady and he knelt down in front of it. There were people everywhere, large crowds of every kind of nationality imaginable.

At that point I wandered over to a flat rock about ten yards away from Keith where I sat down for a rest. Then I happened to look up towards the sky for some reason and I could see the sun dancing. I had never seen such a spectacle although I had heard lots of stories about it.

As I stared at it I noticed that I didn't need my sunglasses which was a surprise – there was no obvious glare from it.

Then suddenly I could feel a presence and looked to my left.

Then I could see Our Lady. She was standing, or should I say floating, about four feet away from me – right in front of me – elevated on a white cloud. She was wearing a blue cloak and a white gown. I began to cry.

"Joe," she said to me, "you see me now the way I showed you before. Relax."

I could feel my body heating up. "You must look after Keith for me, Joe. Keith will see me now."

"Okay, Mother," I said, "what should I do?"

She told me to get some shelter under the tree. I walked over to a small tree she had indicated to me which had a small flat rock under it. I sat down. I glanced over to where Keith was. At this stage he was leading the Rosary with a group of people, his face fixed on Our Lady's Statue.

After about fifteen minutes, during which time Our

Lady gave me a number of personal messages, she said to me: "Go and get Keith now – I am ready to receive him."

I walked over to him and just as I got close the Rosary finished.

"Keith, how are you doing?" I said.

He looked at me with a big smile on his face and he said: "I am waiting to see Our Lady."

"Come with me, Keith," I said, my voice full of emotion. "Over this way. Our Lady is waiting to see you over here."

I brought him over to the flat rock. I told him where to stand and I stood behind him.

"Our Lady is now ready to receive you, Keith," I told him. "Now open your heart."

With that I looked away because this was a private moment for him. My gaze wandered over to the mountains in the far distance. I could see the sun move around the mountains slowly. Then, what looked like a pink ball of light from the sun darted forward and appeared right in front of Keith.

Just then Keith dropped heavily to his knees, so suddenly I jumped back.

He began to speak with Our Lady and cry out loud: "Thank you, Mother, for speaking to me! I waited all my life for this moment. You are beautiful, Mother!" Then, at least three or four times he cried, "I love you, Mother!"

Then Our Lady asked me to leave them for a while. I did this and stood looking away from them. But I couldn't resist for long. I looked over at them again. All I could see was a marshmallow-pink haze surrounding Keith, glowing and shining. Because Our Lady was transparent I could see this vision of Keith clearly.

Then I put my head down, overcome with joy for Keith and the experience he was having with Our Blessed Mother. He was with Our Lady for about ten minutes.

When it was over, Keith, buzzing with excitement, insisted that we go back to the statute and say another decade of the Rosary! So we did.

We went for a walk after that and had a coffee in a local café where we sat for ages discussing what had happened and what Our Lady had said.

That's when I told him that Our Lady had said to me: "Keith has to take you to Knock. You both must go but it is Keith who must take you when he is ready. I will make myself known."

Keith then told me that Our Lady had asked him to go to Knock once a week on his return to Ireland and asked him to pray the Rosary every day from then onwards.

Stunned and shocked, but filled with absolute joy, we tried to make sense of it all as we turned our minds and expectations towards Knock, Ireland's most important Marian Shrine.

Most Irish Catholics know the story of Knock but let me give a brief summary here.

On August 21st 1879, in the evening, an apparition of Our Lady, St Joseph, and a figure taken to be St John the Evangelist appeared on the south gable of Knock Parish Church. To their left was an altar on which was a cross and a lamb with angels swirling around. This apparition was seen by fifteen people, ranging in age from six years to seventy-five. The Blessed Virgin Mary was clothed in white, with a white cloak fastened at the neck. The crown was pale gold, with sparkling decorations on the upper part of it. On her forehead, at the edge of the crown, she wore a golden rose. Her hands and eyes were raised towards Heaven. St Joseph's robes were also white. St John was dressed in white vestments and wore a bishop's mitre on his head. He had an open book in his left hand. The witnesses stood there in pouring rain for two hours, reciting the Rosary. During this time no rain fell on the church gable and the ground in front of it stayed dry. An Ecclesiastical Commission of Inquiry was set up by the Archbishop of Tuam and the final verdict was that the testimony of all the witnesses was trustworthy.

Today Knock is an international place of pilgrimage where over one and a half million pilgrims come every year and now Keith and I were about to join their number.

We were full of anticipation about Knock but were still regretful to leave Medjugorje. Our time there was so special. The feeling of peace, love and joy is difficult for many people to fathom. It is only when you go

Joe arriving at Knock 31st October 2009. *(Photo © Brian Farrell)*

Joe in the Basilica Church on 31st October 2009. *(Photo © Photocall Ireland)*

Joe in the Basilica Church on 31st October 2009. *(Photo © Photocall Ireland)*

Photograph taken in the Knock Apparition Chapel on the 31st October 2009.

Joe and supporter being escorted from Knock Shrine, Co. Mayo. 31st October 2009.
(Photo © Photocall Ireland)

Thousands of people from Ireland and abroad gathered in the grounds of Knock Shrine, Co. Mayo. 31st October 2009 *(Photo © Photocall Ireland)*

Joe's fellow visionary the late Keith Henderson.

Joe and Keith in Medjugorje in 2009.

there that you realise you are in a very special place. We were so privileged to have experienced this. I will never forget the time when we boarded the plane on the way home. Looking around I could see people with tears in their eyes, including myself and Keith. Medjugoje is so special that people don't want to leave.

Indeed, after Medjugorje I was a different man. My faith was fully restored. I began to go to Mass and receive Holy Communion every day, spend one hour in prayer and meditation, say the Rosary daily and attend Benediction.

First Apparition at Knock

Keith went to Knock on our return from Medjugorje. I waited, as Our Lady had instructed, until Keith felt it was time to take me.

After his visit, this is what Keith revealed to me:

"I went to Knock for the first time and I saw the face of Mother's statue turning into real flesh. I got a shock and she asked me, right there and then, to be one of her visionaries for Knock. I ran out of the church crying and blessed myself with holy water. I was trembling with shock yet I felt overwhelmed with joy. I asked her, 'How am I going to do this?' Then she said to me, 'My sweet child, I won't ask you to do anything that you cannot do.' She kept speaking to me every day after that. She speaks in a really sweet, young voice. Nothing but love comes out of her voice and your heart gets filled with so much joy it is hard to describe."

Apparition at Knock August 2009

Keith finally took me to Knock in August 2009. With a group of ten people from Dublin we headed to Knock on a bus.

There, not only did Our Lady appear to us, but unusual activity was witnessed by everyone. Some people saw lots of colours from the sun and others reported seeing a series of three crosses in the sky. All of this lasted for about fifteen minutes. We couldn't keep from staring at the sky, totally mesmerised and shocked to see what was happening in front of us.

I received a message from Our Lady on that day that another apparition was going to take place at Knock two months later on October 11th. This was the message she gave me at that time:

> *"I want all my children to go to Confession and to get reconciliation from my Son Jesus to be able to experience the pure essence of God's love which He has for all His children. This apparition is to communicate a message to all religions. I will communicate many more times*

to my children at my beloved Knock. The Church must listen. I call on them to pray for help to show more grace and mercy to my children. I want to bring faith, joy, peace and happiness back into the lives of my children in these terrible times.

"I want my statue brought into the church with my visionaries walking behind. I ask that one of my priests recite the Rosary in the church at 3 p.m. When the Rosary is finished I will make myself known to all of my children who come to me with an open heart. I will give my visionary Keith a message for all of my children. I want my message to be given to my children. My priests will accommodate my visionaries this time."

Apparition at Kerrytown, September 29th 2009

During the summer of 2009 Our Lady had communicated to me that she would make herself known at Kerrytown on Tuesday, September 29th. I contacted the group of people in the locality who had attended a healing service with me in Dungloe previously.

When the time came, I travelled there. Keith was unable to attend.

We gathered at the statue of the Virgin Mary at the Rock and began to say the Rosary.

What happened next was truly miraculous. Our Lady appeared and spoke to me but the others also witnessed the most amazing phenomena. A series of crosses appeared in the sky, one replacing another. This went on for about ten minutes. Then the group saw the white statue with its red heart begin to change. Our Lady's head turned and she looked down at the children who were at the front of the group. She began to cry and one woman went up to dry the tears that were running down from her eyes. Witnesses in Kerrytown later gave their accounts to a reporter from the *Irish Independent* and to Highland Radio.

Apparition at Knock, October 11th 2009

We went to Knock on Sunday, October 11th 2009, as Our Lady had instructed. After the Rosary was said in the Apparition Chapel at 3 p.m. she appeared. The event was witnessed by up to 5000 people.

Many people had found out about it because I did a number of radio interviews explaining about the apparition in advance. I had also informed the Shrine office in Knock in advance. Throngs of people began to arrive early that day. By noon, the car parks were overflowing to such a degree that people began to abandon their cars wherever they could find a spot – even far out on the roads leading into Knock. Men, women and children, they walked the rest of the way.

People gathered outside the south gable of Knock Old Parish Church, the original chapel built after the Apparitions of 1879, as they could not get into the chapel itself because it was full.

I should explain that in Knock there are three main places of public worship. The largest is the Basilica which is used to accommodate thousands of people during annual pilgrimages. It is closed during the winter. The normal everyday church is Knock Old Parish Church. This is where Mass is said for locals and others on a daily basis. Then there is the Apparition Chapel which is at the gable end of the old church and is covered with a large ceiling-to-floor glass window and is used for those who want to say the Rosary there every day. Mass is never said here.

Representatives of Knock Shrine, including the priests, made a concerted effort to block visitors who had come specifically to witness the apparition, other than those "authorised" as part of the annual pilgrimage, from entering the main and larger Basilica. And they succeeded.

Meanwhile, thc parish priest's calls to the "organised" group of pilgrims to come into the Basilica fell on deaf ears. Word had got to the pilgrims from the crowds that the apparition was to happen. Part of an annual excursion, they remained firmly seated outside the Old Chapel and refused to move.

In the Apparition Chapel, Keith and I were kneeling at the altar in front of the statute of Our Lady and we began to say the Rosary. The entire chapel recited the

Holy Rosary out loud and we could hear the large crowd outside the chapel join in. There was an incredible comradeship that day with so many people saying the Rosary in unison.

Immediately after the Rosary I felt Our Lady's presence and began to cry (this is always how I know she is near). I looked up then and saw her standing in front of me but floating, elevated at least three feet from the base of the statue. She seemed to have emerged slowly from the statue into a bright dazzling image where she appeared to be in full human form, flesh and blood. She seemed to be moving the entire time, as if a wind was blowing all around her. She was wearing a pale blue cloak with a white shimmering gown underneath. I could not see her feet. She had a sweet smile but it looked somewhat sad.

As soon as she gave me the message she smiled again and told me to tell the people to look up at the sky where she would give a sign to everyone there.

I struggled outside holding the large wooden cross we had taken in with us earlier and made my way towards the small mound of grass that lies opposite the gable wall of the Apparition Chapel.

This was around 3.20 p.m. and it was then that I could hear people begin to shout, "Look up at the sun! Look up at the sun!"

As soon as we heard people shouting, we stopped abruptly and looked up at the sky. The sun was dancing. We stood still, gazing upwards, marvelling at the way Our Lady had shown a sign as she had promised.

People screamed, "Look, the sun has changed! It's dancing! Look, it's jumping all over the place! Can you see the black ring around it?"

One woman from Dublin, Emma Maughan, who travelled to Knock with her two daughters, told me later that she had come with an open mind and out of curiosity. She told me her story afterwards. According to her, as she glanced upwards the sun changed colour to a bright metallic shade and began to jump from side to side. She said, "Normally it is not possible to stare at the sun for more than two seconds without glancing away. But on that day, the sun changed its colour, tone and glare so that it was possible to watch it without having to look away, because the usual glare, where no one could possibly look into the sun, was dull. It looked as though a silver metallic disc had been placed over the sun. It started to spin and rock from side to side and then disappear into the clouds. This sequence took place for fifteen minutes, during which time it repeatedly gyrated, jumped, and flashed in and out before it would disappear into the clouds again. People were taking photos and videos on their cameras and mobile phones. During all of this, press photographers had their cameras pinned on the crowd – not the sky – to take shots of people looking at the sky.

"My daughter, meanwhile, had her video camera rolling the entire time. She thought she had taken shots of the sun dancing, but a strange thing happened in the car on the way home. As we were driving home, about an hour away from Knock, she shouted at me to pull the car over. She started to cry and asked me to look at the video camera footage and tell her what I could see. What I saw shocked me to the core. I saw two images. One featured what I can only describe as the Virgin Mary's face and the other looked like any photo I have seen of Saint Padre Pio."

Meanwhile, Keith Henderson, who had received the message in the church beforehand, spoke to the throngs of people and revealed the message, although it was very difficult to hear him. This message was, however, recorded and a number of people uploaded it on YouTube.

> *"I want to thank all my children for coming to Knock today, especially those who come with an open heart. I want all my children to convert back to my church. There is only one religion and that is my religion.*
>
> *Some of my priests do not show compassion to my children. I want all of my priests to start showing compassion to all of my children, especially those who convert back to my church. I want to bring more peace to Ireland, north and south. Thank you to all my children for responding to my call today."*

After that day the media coverage was extensive. Not just in Ireland but across the world, so I have been told. Many people discussed what they had seen, both in the media and online. Very few, however, were willing to "go public" for fear of being laughed at or ridiculed. I believe that, since then, more and more people are prepared to come forward and bear witness to the truth.

There was a mixed reaction from the media – some of it was just straight reporting while other articles went to great trouble to pour scorn and come up with creative headlines that were both insulting and completely misleading. I was painted as a fraud, a scam artist and other more scurrilous titles. I had realised before this that I could expect this kind of reaction and that I would just have to get used to it. It's a cross I have to bear. But in fairness to the media, it's not every day, let's face it, that someone comes out with the claims that I made. It's not every day where thousands of people witness an extraordinary event such as a dancing sun! So how they reacted was as I would have expected them to.

Second Apparition at Knock, October 31st 2009

In the lead-up the next apparition, I went through a tough, challenging time where some of the media questions put to me were so insulting that I was completely taken aback. Now that I was in the media light, I would be questioned, scrutinised and laughed at constantly.

It was during this period that every day, when I said the Holy Rosary in my prayer room at 3 p.m., I would receive a different message from Our Lady. I wouldn't see her but she would speak to me. Most of these were loving, private messages. Then she made it very clear to me that she wanted everyone – as many people as possible to know about the next apparition. And so, once again, details were sent to the media in Ireland.

It was during these daily messages in the lead-up to October 31st that Our Lady told me that she would "rock" the foundations of the Church on the day of the next apparition and that she would "make herself known". I have come to realise that every time she refers to "making herself known", she means she will give a public sign of her presence.

As soon as I sent out the notice to the press about the next apparition, the media frenzy began again. As I expected this I welcomed it. I agreed to almost every media interview I was asked to do. But because there were so many, I couldn't get to all the ones I would have liked. Apart from the Irish interviews, I did one for BBC Radio 4 in advance of the apparitions of October 31st. I reckon this is why so many people came from abroad for this apparition.

The publicity side of things was frightening for me, as I was not used to dealing with the media. I thought, naïvely, that they would just listen and leave it for people to make up their own minds. But I know now that this is not the case. I can't say I was shown any kind of respect with the exception of a few impartial reporters who wanted to hear my side.

What I found particularly saddening was the negative reaction from the people who run Knock shrine. I realise, though, that they have to keep an open mind on such things but that didn't stop the hurt I felt when the Apparition of Our Lady was denied outright. No, it wasn't happening, they said. It was all in people's imagination. What an insult to those people who were there and saw it all for themselves. How can thousands of people be wrong? But, of course, they said that in Fatima too when 70,000 people claimed to have witnessed the sun dancing. So some things simply never change. We were all "deluded" according to these people who, to this day, still hold the same view.

Either way, I was unprepared for the huge response when between 8000 and 10,000 people showed up at Knock on October 31st 2010. I had warned the people at Knock to be prepared for a big crowd. They knew that up to 10,000 people would show up because we had contacted them in advance so that they knew what to expect. We had also requested access to the Basilica but had been warned that it was the end of the season and that more than likely it would not be open. When Keith and I arrived, we were met by the media. I welcomed this. Even if some of them were openly abusive to me, it didn't matter. The word, I felt, was at last getting out. People were sitting up and listening. So this was something I realised I would have to accept.

On the day I arrived, I had been warned, once again, by Knock representatives that they would not be opening up the Basilica, that this was only "used for official pilgrims". That's when people could hear the media arguments made by them which included, "This is not how Our Lady works"; "She never predicts apparitions in advance"; "She only comes to small groups of people". The arguments put forward by the Church were also negative.

The Archbishop of Tuam, Dr Michael Neary, made very clear the church's view of my predictions immediately after the apparition on October 11th 2009.

> *"It is not healthy, does not give glory to God and certainly is not good witness to the faith to be looking for extraordinary phenomena. The apparition of 1879 was neither sought nor expected by the humble, honest people who were its astonished witnesses . . . Unfortunately, recent events at the Shrine obscure this essential message. They risk misleading God's people and undermining faith. For this reason such events are to be regretted rather than encouraged."*

So, if the original apparitions, which took place in 1879, are "the real thing", what test did they have to pass to be considered such? The Church claims that such apparitions need to be scrutinised and treated with extreme caution. While the Catholic Church permits us to believe in supernatural occurrences – the Immaculate Conception, the Resurrection and other "miracles" – it seems they don't accept or believe in modern-day miracles. Not only do they doubt such revelations, but they also don't provide any spiritual guidance to the many people who have borne witness to such recent apparitions.

The sceptical and moral stance adopted by Church representatives against what was happening was made very clear. The Church did not explain why they took this view. They just decided to condemn the events outright. No room here for keeping an open mind. Of course, if it took almost thirty years for the Catholic Church to set up a commission to investigate Medjugorje, then what happened in Knock is not surprising.

Though we had been told the Basilica would not be opened that day, they were obliged to open it because of the huge number of people present. But before we entered it, we were told emphatically that the statue of Our Lady, which is usually wheeled into the church for all pilgrimages, would not be brought in on this occasion. This, we were once again reminded, was not an "official" pilgrimage. It didn't matter to them that up to 10,000 people had shown up, an enormous feat when you consider the rapid drop in the number of people attending Catholic churches in Ireland at the time! Then it became apparent that the microphones had been removed, as had the Holy Host. We didn't let that deter us.

Kneeling in front of the altar, it was hard not to notice the number of flashing cameras in my face. Some photographers, to get a better view, pointed their cameras right in front of my nose.

There were so many people behind me that I felt I was being pushed every few seconds. Despite the distraction and the heaving of the crowds around me, I finally settled down.

Then the Rosary began – and proceeded with difficulty as there were no microphones and it was impossible to get that huge number of people to make the responses in unison.

I waited. And then the tears began. I always cry but they are tears of joy. It's what Our Lady calls the gift of tears. No sooner do I cry than I feel her presence. It's instantaneous. As soon as this happens, my head snaps back. I stare ahead in silence for a few minutes before she appears in all her glory.

That day, she was again dressed in a white robe and flowing blue mantle, smelling of sweet roses as she usually does. Then she smiled so sweetly at me, I felt I was being taken out of my body, carried at the speed of light onto another plane. It was then, to my absolute amazement, that I was shown another vision of Heaven. At first, the light was so blinding and hot that I couldn't look at it directly. Then Our Lady told me in the sweetest voice, *"Joe, my dear child, look at the Light. It will give you strength. Courage!"*

It was like being in a dream state. I knew my body was down in the church but my spirit had left. I was in a room. Then she placed me before a white marble altar on which lay a beautiful little white lamb – a real baby lamb. She told me to kneel before it. I knew in my heart that it represented Jesus, the Lamb of God. The lamb seemed to have had its throat cut, and I could see the red line of blood, but not flowing. Yet the lamb didn't seem to be in any pain. Nor was it dying. I knew that she was trying to give me a message to show that Jesus, the Lamb of God, had been sacrificed for the sins of the world.

I was then presented with a white chalice that seemed to be made completely out of light. To my utter amazement, this was handed to me by Jesus Himself. This beautiful young handsome man. His rich brown shoulder-length hair, sallow skin and white robe was an image I had seen before in many of my visions and during my near death experience. Yet every time, his deep, startling, piercing blue eyes, which contrast so starkly with his sallow skin, penetrate every part of my being with such utter tenderness and love that it's incomparable to anything you could experience on this Earth.

Our Lady asked me to drink of the chalice. I held it in my hands but I couldn't feel it, yet I knew it was there and that I was meant to drink from it. I drank and it was like a white cloudy liquid. I could feel it as it trickled slowly into my body. I immediately felt my entire being infused with incredible energy, light and healing, and enveloped with a love that is beyond human comprehension.

Suddenly I was back – back in my body at the altar in the Basilica in Knock, surrounded by thousands of people. But I didn't see anyone – only Our Lady, the Blessed Mother of Jesus. She was speaking to me. She was all I could hear.

Then I heard the bang from the roof of the church and I came to. At first I thought it was a roll of thunder. But as it was repeated, I saw that people were running out of the church and that a stampede had started towards the back. Then people started to shout, "Outside, quick. Look at the sun! It's spinning. It's dancing!"

Drained after the apparition in the Church, I stayed where I was and continued to pray.

I did not go outside until much later, as I was still in prayer, but this is an account of what happened next.

One woman, Kathleen Ruddy, told me afterwards: "I ran outside the church and noticed everyone looking up and pointing at the sun. As I looked up, I noticed that it was a deep golden colour, but I could look at it. It had a sort of hazy frosted front and it keep gyrating and spinning. I was rooted to the ground with shock. I couldn't believe what I was seeing. It looked like it was rocking from side to side, dazzling, changing size, reducing size and then increasing again. In and out of the clouds it went.

"Then suddenly I saw a sight that left me stunned. Three crosses appeared in the sky, clearly. There was no doubt in my mind what I was seeing. Open-mouthed, I looked to my right and saw a woman taking photos on her mobile phone. She looked back at me and her eyes told me that we were both witnessing a miracle, but we were too shocked, too speechless to even communicate this fact.

"Then I saw the face of a woman to the right of the sun. It was a large image of a woman's face. I knew instantly that it was an image of Our Lady. I burst into tears. I couldn't take in what I was seeing. It was all too much. Then I saw what I thought was an image of Jesus on the Cross. I could hear people moaning in the background but had no interest. My gaze was fixed firmly on the sky. All of this spectacle lasted over twenty-five minutes. I was instantly converted. Converted once and for all – for life. Although a Roman Catholic I had not practised for many years and was very unsure as to whether to believe in God or not. I felt the most amazing freedom, a freedom I never thought possible on this Earth, the freedom that comes from finally knowing the truth: that God exists, freedom from the fear of death. All of the fear just left me. And in its place this wonderful sense of pure relief as well as freedom. Because now I didn't have any more doubts. That's a great feeling, believe you me."

Myself and Keith managed to get a quick glimpse of the sun spinning in the sky but due to the amount of people surrounding us we had to get away quickly. We had to be taken out of the car park in a security van which, in fairness to the Knock Shrine management, had to be organised at the last minute for our safety. When we managed to get out of the car park and away, Keith and I sat down in front of three witnesses in the house of a friend of Keith's and recounted the following messages we had both received at Knock, from Our Blessed Mother on that day, October 31st 2009. All of the witnesses signed the messages.

The following is the message I received from Our Lady that day:

> *"Thank you for responding to my call. I am so happy. I smile on this day, 31 October 2009, at my beloved Knock. I wish to thank all the people who came today to pray, to give thanks to my beloved Father God the Almighty. I am the Immaculate Heart, Mother of all my children, Mother of all God's children. I am the Immaculate Conception. I am Queen of the Heavens. I am Queen of the Earth. I will glorify my Father's name through prayer from the people who come to pray. I ask for conversion many times. I ask for peace. I ask for prayers every day for my son's apostles. I pray that they*

will listen. I pray and I ask for unification of the faith across the globe. I pray that this message has been listened to. That is has been given around the globe in different ways to all my faithful. I thank all my children today for responding. I will visit one day soon on the fifth day of the Holy Month. Peace be with you, my children."

The following is the message received by Keith Henderson at Knock on October 31st 2009:

"I love all my children unconditionally with my Immaculate Heart, especially all my priests who are not listening to my call. I ask all my children to pray for my priests. Pray. Pray. Pray."

Keith Henderson also went on record to predict the next apparition, before the same witnesses, saying that the next apparition would take place on December fifth 2009 in the Basilica at Knock and that the Rosary was to be said at 3 p.m.

What the media did not seem to understand, once we published that message, was that Our Lady did not claim this time that "she would make herself known". In fact, Keith and I did not really recognise the significance of that at first. But, after much discussion we realised that this was to be a private apparition, similar to the ones which take place in Medjugorje, where the public don't necessarily see any outward sign. But the press came anyway, expecting another apparition where the sun danced in the sky, only it didn't happen.

When we knelt down it was very difficult. We had a TV camera in our face and quite a number of photographers – I don't know where half of them had come from – were clicking away. It was really distracting. Nevertheless, once Keith and I began to recite the Rosary we finally went into channel as we expected. There were not many in the church that day because I had deliberately kept the news of it out of the media once I realised it was to be a private apparition. But because we had published the date immediately after the last apparition more people turned up than we had anticipated.

But when the media reported that apparition, their headlines screamed: "*No Show of Our Lady at Knock*". The irony of it made me smile. Did this mean that they actually believed in the miracle of the sun, in the first instance, which was witnessed by many people on October 31st at Knock?

But show she did, to myself and Keith.

Her message was to me was this:

"Hello, my dear Joseph.

"Thank you for coming today.

"I am happy you have responded to my call. You are very much loved by God and all God's angels. Love, my dear child, is the greatest gift God has bestowed upon all of His children, especially on you, my child. Do not worry. You are very much protected. No harm will come to you. I have placed my most powerful mantle all around my children today especially my children who have responded to my call.

"All here today have been covered with the Holy Spirit. My beloved Son, Jesus, is very happy today. My dear Joseph, tell my children to pray from their hearts. They must pray for all of our priests. Pray. Pray.

"I am most happy when my children pray. Pray for peace. Pray for conversion. Pray for understanding. Pray for mercy. Pray for grace. Pray that the Devil stays away from the Church. Pray that the Devil loses his power over God's people. Pray to my beloved Son, Jesus the Christ for guidance and He will help you. Pray every day to St Michael for protection against the snares of the Devil. Pray for your persecution to be lifted. You must pray every day, my child. For prayer is the most powerful weapon against the darkness. Conversion is beginning. I am happy. It will take time. I will visit in the year 2010 at the

Apparition Chapel at 3pm on Sunday 10th January 2010.

"Bless you, my child.

"Mary, Mother of Jesus."

She also had a message for Keith:

"The Roman Catholic Church must listen to my children – our majestic seers. They all must heed the important information. The messages that have been given are and have always been authentic. I implore you, my dear children, to listen. To listen with your heart. The disciples of my beloved son Jesus must be respected and prayed for every day.

"Respect must come from within the House of God – our beloved Father, Creator and Lord of all creation past, present, and to come.

"The Holy Eucharist, my child, is the real presence of the risen Christ in Heaven and also here on Earth – the Body, the Blood, the Soul and Divinity. My children must kneel when receiving the Holy Eucharist as the angels do in Heaven. My dear Child Jesus, my beloved Son, with the whole church offers public worship to the eternal Father.

"Thank you for your time and for responding to my call.

"Mother of Heaven, Queen of the Angels, Mother of Jesus, Mother of peace and love."

Description of Our Lady

At this point I feel I must refer to Our Lady in more detail. I am so used to seeing her now that, from time to time, I take it all for granted. So many people are curious and anxious to know much more about her than just the messages she gives to me.

People constantly ask, when meeting me for the first time, "What does Our Lady look like, Joe?" And I give them the same answer time and time again. I see her with my heart first.

But what *does* Our Lady look like? There are no words that would do her justice. I get a lump in my throat when I think of her and my insides turn into putty.

She is beautiful beyond comprehension. Our human minds simply are not open enough to absorb this kind of pure, surreal beauty. When I see Our Lady, I see her as pure love. Very gentle. Very kind. Very loving.

Always, every single time, she appears to me just as a loving mother would come to her child. Not as "Our Lady, Mother of God", but as a real mother. It feels as if she puts her arms around me like any mother would do with her a very much-loved child. It's such a fantastic, wonderful feeling.

Our Lady has given me the gift of tears. I cry the minute I feel her presence, before she appears to me. That's how I always know it is really her. Every single time. That's when I know she's real, when she has arrived. Other people I know who have been fortunate to see her also get the exact same feeling. They feel tears first before they see her.

Nevertheless, the first thing I now do when I see her is to ask, "Mother, please tell me where you come from and who you are?" And she will say, "*I come from the Light. The Light of God. The Most High. I come in God's Holy Name. I am the Mother of Jesus the Christ.*" Or she will say, "*I am Queen of the Heavens*" or "*I am Queen of the Angels*"; "*I am Queen of Knock*"; "*I am a Messenger for God*"; "*I am the Immaculate Conception*"; and similar titles. She gives herself different titles, depending on the message. I always ask her to identify herself first, for many reasons. The first is because the Prince of Darkness, the Evil One, can manifest himself as an angel. But no evil spirit will ever say they are from the Light. Ever. It's sad that I have to do this, but absolutely necessary.

She is tall, slim, very feminine, dark-haired and young. She is always standing upright but never at ground level; she tends to always be above it so that you are looking upwards the whole time. She floats over a thick mist of white cloud, with roses in red, gold and other mysterious glowing colours around her feet. I immediately get a strong smell of roses from her.

Her smile is dazzling. She always, always, speaks to me before she smiles. "Welcome, my sweet child," she says. Then she opens her arms out, palms relaxed but facing upwards. She wears a blue cloak which opens out to reveal a white robe, right down to her feet. It flows and is not belted. I always see her toes and a little part of her feet, which are bare.

Her veil is sky-blue, the same colour as her cloak; she calls it her holy mantle. I can see a small strand of hair peeping out of her veil and sometimes around the sides of her face. Her rich brown hair is not very long and only reaches below her jawbone.

Never still, she seems to be always moving, "waving" in slow motion, and her clothes blow in a soft wind. Her beautiful large eyes are a startling, piercing blue. Love and light shines from her eyes and a glow of light flows from the palms of her hands.

Her skin is beautiful, like a newborn baby's – not one blemish – like delicate porcelain. There is a slight rose tint on her cheeks and on her lips. Her lips are thin but very pretty.

When she appears, she is in the flesh; she is actually alive. I see her just as I would anyone else.

What does she sound like? Her voice sounds like that of a young woman but so gentle and pure. Her voice is clear, audible, but not loud – but more than a whisper.

When I look at her, I always tell her how much I love her and how beautiful she is. Then she often reveals her heart to demonstrate her love. This appears like a human heart. I can see it pulsating – but I don't see valves or blood or anything like that. It is surrounded by a pink mist. I have since learned, as I have got to know her, understand her, and develop a close relationship with her, that this is her sign of unconditional love that shines down on me. And not just on me – it's for all her children. She never fails to smile when I see her. Sometimes, though, she is sad and tears can pour down her cheeks.

How do I talk to her? People assume that I see her only at the public apparitions. This is not the case. I began to see her physically more easily than I did before in January and February 2010. I find, now, that I can go into "channel" much faster. And it can be anywhere, but it is usually in a quiet place.

As soon as I enter a church now, or kneel down to say the Holy Rosary, I can go into channel and call her if the Holy Spirit moves me to do so. It cannot be "done on demand" and it must be done in absolute quiet prayer and reflection. It must be completely from the heart.

I bless myself and take out my beads. I then tell her, "I am here today, Mother. I need to speak with you." I feel her presence before I see or hear her. I get goose pimples first. My arms and hands shake just before she comes. I get this incredible feeling around me, like a cloak being placed around my shoulders. Then the tears come. Very often, I see an image of the crucifix before she comes.

I used to think that she only appeared when I would stare at her statue. She has since told me, *"Joe, don't stare at my statue. People will say this is idolatry."*

"Okay, Mother, so what do you want me to do?" I ask her.

"Look at where your heart takes you."

The last couple of times in Knock I saw her emerge not from the statue but from above the altar. This was a new experience for me and it has given me more confidence, because I realise that when I call her now, in the right circumstances, she will appear to me either in person or I will hear her wherever I am.

Our Lady's Role

Many Christians ask me why Our Lady is so powerful. Surely I should be praying to Jesus Christ directly? Our Lady has no real role – has she? Am I not guilty of idolatry – replacing Jesus with Our Lady?

Our Lady has explained this to me time and time again. She has been sent by God, not of her own accord. She is his Divine Messenger, with special authority to bring people closer to God. She has a pivotal role to play in helping God in the redemption of the human race before the Second Coming of Christ on Earth.

The Time is at Hand

The time has finally come. We don't need Our Lady's words to convince us that belief in God, the supreme being, is virtually collapsing. In its wake comes the biggest spiritual war of all time, a war that is not only glaringly obvious but one which has been prophesied for many centuries now. And all of it is contained in the Bible and, in particular, the Book of Revelation which up to December 2009 I had never read before in my life. Now it all makes sense.

God told us in the Bible that a spiritual war would erupt close to the time he would return to the Earth. I believe that time is now very near – as close as two years if not sooner. The race has already begun.

Right now, as I write this, a worldwide attack on the validity of Christianity is being mounted by Satan and his army to continue to destroy people's faith. He has convinced people to dispute the teachings of the Holy Bible, God's divine revelation to the world. "The Holy Book" as Our Lady describes it to me, contains the Truth – the truth about the purpose of human life on Earth and the truth as to how we should live our lives to fulfil the purpose for which we were put on the Earth. It is all a big test. Make no mistake. And it has been written, as Our Lady says, "in my Father's Book" that we can choose between the word of God or the lies that Satan spreads. It's up to us. We have our own free will which God cannot, and will not, interfere with. He leaves it up to us.

The Second Coming of Christ on the Earth

The messages I receive from Our Lady have a direct bearing on the Second Coming. Christ, she tells me, is already here on Earth. He walks in Egypt and, at this time, is preparing his followers to herald the Second Coming, when he will make himself known. And this will happen soon. I cannot give an exact date yet because I have not been told.

For most Christians, the Second Coming of Christ, as foretold in the Bible in the Book of Revelations, simply means the return again, on Earth, of Jesus Christ. When he returns, it is expected that the prophecies contained therein will be fulfilled. This is where the dead will be resurrected, those on Earth will be finally judged and the new Kingdom of God on Earth will be fully established. Heaven and Earth will become one.

The message, when broken down to its simplest form, means just one thing: Christ will return again to judge the living and the dead. He will finally and totally wipe out his enemies, led by Satan. All those faithful to His teachings will be blessed with a new Heaven and a new Earth when victory has been achieved.

I don't claim to have the answers. I am simply a messenger for Our Lady. She has shown me visions and will, if I ask her, show me more. But I don't want to see them, not yet. Perhaps in time. Believe me when I say that what I have seen already is too distressing for words. My heart bleeds when I see these visions. I worry for my family, friends and for all of mankind. It has been heartbreaking and very frightening.

I do believe in my heart, though, that it is not all doom and gloom. I believe God is merciful and I believe that it is really up to us all to reconsider our spirituality and acknowledge God. Then and only then will we achieve real peace and happiness on this Earth. This Earth will not die – I know that – it can only get better. But unfortunately, before it does, a lot of world events, some not so good, will definitely happen as part of the global "cleansing" that Our Lady keeps referring to.

Before I received the messages from Our Lady, I had, I am embarrassed to admit, not read the Bible, other than extracts read out at Mass on Sundays. However, I have since, with the help of a few friends, begun to dig into the various interpretations of Paul's messages to the Thessalonians. It immediately became clear that there are various views, some of which contradict each other, as to how the prophecies will be fulfilled.

The Rapture

The Bible refers to the day that the Lord comes back:

> *We who are alive on the day the Lord comes will not go ahead of those who have died. There will be the shout of command, the archangel's voice, the sound of God's trumpet, and the Lord himself will*

come down from Heaven. Those who have died believing will be gathered up along with them in the clouds to meet the Lord in the air. And so we will always be with the Lord. (1 Thessalonians 4)

This is supported in other passages.

Tribulation

There are three theories. Many people believe that the Rapture will happen just *before* the expected seven-year "Tribulation", when there will be a desperate time of great suffering, instability, and the predicted War of Armageddon, when the largest genocide ever seen in the world will take place. Some believe that it will happen just *after* the Tribulation, when Jesus finally returns to Earth. Others suggest that those people without sin and with great faith will be "lifted" off the Earth while the remaining sinners will be left behind.

I know that God, through Our Lady, is trying to prepare us in two ways. For those who believe in God, Our Lady urges us to pray for others in order to save their souls. For those who have lost their belief, she asks them to keep an open mind and consider the possibility that God does, in fact, exist. She says that Jesus Christ loves everyone and will accept with open arms all those who "see the light", even at the last minute.

The Final Day

It has been made absolutely clear in the Bible, in the second letter of St Paul to the Thessalonians, that the Final Day won't come about "*until the final rebellion takes place and the Wicked One appears who is destined for Hell. He* [the Anti-Christ] *will oppose every so-called God or object of worship and will put himself above them all. He will even go in and sit down in God's temple and claim to be God.*"

Breakdown of Society

Take one look at the world in which you are living today. Make up your own mind. What do you see? It's a bad place right now. Could the Tribulation have already started? Daily unrest, a rise in vicious, heinous crime, murder, terrorism, an increase in the manufacture of nuclear arms, war, disease, famine, financial disasters, lack of morality, racism, family breakdown, bigotry and an obscene fascination with fake idols, including people, objects and lifestyles. Not a pretty sight. Not a great period to live in, is it?

Celebrity culture, idolatry in it most tacky form, has devoured and consumed our lives and those of our children. So called "models of perfection" are shoved into our face through TV and across internet screens daily, usually when they have been misbehaving themselves in some way. Their dramatic and "screwed-up" lives are broadcast today as headline news stories! These are the role models our children will base their lives on. This is what is meant by idolatry and it has reached epidemic proportions.

Can the number of earthquakes, floods and other natural disasters all be analysed and blamed on climate change? Have you noticed how frequent they have become? Why does everything seem to have gone wrong, unexpectedly and all so suddenly? Few of us, with the exception of the super-rich, can fail to have noticed the way that every single part of our lives has been affected so drastically. From feeding our families to paying our mortgage, to holding down a job, to surviving – it has all passed out of our control.

All of this is played out against a background of dishonesty, greed and corruption in the very financial institutions we set up to safeguard our future. People in their late fifties and sixties can't remember an economic slump as sinister as the current one. Older people, while they do remember the poor periods of the 1930s, 1940s and 1950s, will tell you that people still had their faith then. It got them through it. They, in particular, are reeling with shock and bitter disappointment at the recent scandals in the Catholic Church. Is this what it has come to after all these years?

Yes, I think it's fair to assume that the Tribulation may have already started.

Our Last Chance to Redeem Ourselves

This is precisely why Our Lady is manifesting herself throughout the world, in so many incidents in the last century, to try to prepare us. Sadly, her words have not been listened to and the number of sceptics continues to rise.

Through the mystery of the Holy Rosary, which she says will offer us all the powerful protection we need in our fight against the Evil One, she will lead the world towards salvation, with God's believers – his army of loyal followers – in tow.

She has told me that she was chosen by God to fight the Evil One after the birth of her Son Jesus. God permitted her to protect Jesus while he was here on the Earth, as he was constantly under attack by Satan. She knew in her lifetime that she was going to be made Queen of Heaven and Earth one day.

She has reminded me time and time again to remember her Son's words before he left this Earth: "*He who believes in me shall live forever. He shall not die.*" And this is why, she says, she is making herself known more and more throughout the world. It is why God has asked her to send us signs – signs that will make us sit up and take note. She is seeking conversion in order that we can live forever in God's Kingdom. We have one last chance to redeem ourselves before the Second Coming. Our last chance will be July 10th 2015. This is not to be confused with the date of the Second Coming, which is not known, nor will it be, in advance. No, it is the last chance we get for redeeming ourselves in the eyes of God.

Although full of love and mercy, God is not prepared to stand idly by and let Satan rule the hearts of His children. The hand of God will come down now, she says. He may be the God of love but He will no longer tolerate what's happening in the world. He will not allow his children to continue with a life of evil and destruction. The Wrath of God is very close, she tells me. And that time is now drawing nearer.

In her messages, which she wants broadcast around the world, she is expecting an instant response this time. There is panic on Earth, she says. Now is the time for her, as a messenger from God, to communicate with all people on Earth through human communication. She wants the world to be converted through the signs and messages she will impart. And this has to be done through modern communications. She is gathering believers everywhere in the world to prepare for the Second Coming.

She claims that there are more visionaries than ever in the world now. In 1980, she says, millions of angels sent from heaven were born. Now around thirty years of age, they are her key "Light workers" on Earth. All are gathering in strength now to do God's work in defending the Earth against Satan.

These special chosen souls have been brought into

the world to help cleanse the Earth for a reason – to bring powerful energy back to the Earth.

Why does she appear only to some? She appears only to those souls that were put here for a purpose – those who have been given work to do for her.

10

Light Workers

It is now recognised by psychics and seers all over the world that God, in his quest to teach people the importance of our spiritual life, has sent thousands of "Light workers" into the world. I realised this many years ago. These have increased in number as the Second Coming draws nearer. They have been sent to spread the good news and to show people the meaning of life, not only on this Earth but on the other side. Some call them "Angels of the Light".

Natural channels of spirit, Light workers have come to Earth with one purpose only – to spread the Light and the Truth through love and spiritual healing. Their role is to spread peace, harmony and an understanding of the higher universal plane and angelic realm. Originally angels but now become human, they have been sent to Earth to fight evil. Assisted closely by God's angels, they are devoted to serving others. Their mission in life is to spread kindness and love, to "lighten" people's lives and to help open up people's connection with their natural spiritual selves beyond the physical realm.

In a nutshell, they help people to understand the sixth sense – the psychic sense that is outside of the five senses of sight, hearing, touch, smell and taste. They are here to encourage those of us whose beliefs are firmly rooted in the scientific "wisdom" of the world to look beyond, to bring us all closer to our inner spiritual selves through different forms of teaching and healing.

Blessed with numerous special gifts, they are now, more than at any other time, set to create a huge influence in the world, and to bring a new breed of believers into the "Light" through their healing powers.

Where Do They Come From?

They come from spirit. God is spirit. They come from the universal divine power that comes from God – the maker of all things. Yet they don't represent organised "religion", which is man-made. They work with the very essence of God's pure love. Part of the divine plan, they have been sent from Heaven to keep the human race "on their toes" by helping them tap their spiritual selves. Many of them are blessed with psychic skills and possess special powers that even they don't fully realise until they reach their thirties. Their spiritual healing gifts have been given to them to fight evil and negativity in the world today.

Each Light worker volunteered to come to Earth and picked his or her human identity in advance. They chose the families they were born into. Many of them were born in 1980 and others in the millennium. I personally know of about forty Light workers who were born in the year 1980, which was the year when the majority of Light workers actively working in the world today were sent to Earth. They are not what I would call "madly" religious. While some of them would attend church regularly, others wouldn't. Many people refer to their origins as coming from a divine realm, a higher plane or similar. Some refer loosely to the power that "some people" call God as the source of all things. But make no mistake, they are part of the divine revelation of God on this Earth. God *is* love. And that is central to their core being.

How Can we Identify Them?

Sensitive by nature, they are considered to have a "big heart" and sometimes can be taken for granted by others – even taken advantage of. A little shy when you meet them first, they are really just gentle souls with everyone's interests at heart. Drawn to helping other people overcome obstacles, they are always the first to lend a hand if you are in trouble. They rarely put themselves first.

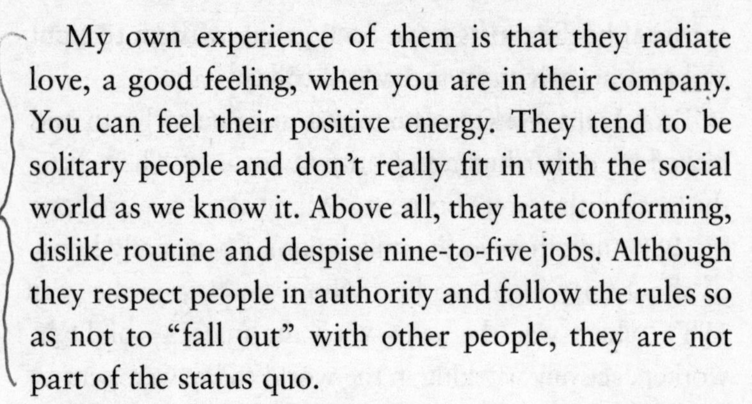

My own experience of them is that they radiate love, a good feeling, when you are in their company. You can feel their positive energy. They tend to be solitary people and don't really fit in with the social world as we know it. Above all, they hate conforming, dislike routine and despise nine-to-five jobs. Although they respect people in authority and follow the rules so as not to "fall out" with other people, they are not part of the status quo.

They cannot stand confrontation of any kind. Instead they adopt a gentle approach to achieve their sole objective in this world – to create love, peace and harmony. Born with a natural affinity to identify with human energy around them, they have an extraordinary ability to pick up "vibes" as soon as they meet people. For example, if they walk into a room they can feel a negative energy almost instantly and can pinpoint who exactly in the room it is coming from. Likewise they can pick up on people's integrity, honesty and deviousness in a way that defies human logic. Drawn to spirituality by natural instinct, many of them become energy healers, clergy, religious professionals or psychics.

Without stereotyping them, they appear as "free spirits" and hate wearing traditional clothes that conform to society. Instead they prefer to walk barefoot when at home, like the outdoors, can tend to be vegetarians (but not always) and love water, rivers, the ocean, as well as forests, mountains and unspoilt countryside.

They love memorabilia. If they are religious they

will have statues, keep a collection of angel cards, books on spirituality, love incense and any book which helps educate them further into a newer understanding of spiritual matters.

How to Know if You are a Light Worker

Often, the first thing that people whom I suspect of being a true Light worker will say to me is "Joe, why do I attract people who are *needy*? What is it about me? Why do they keep coming to me?" I smile, because that is the first inkling they have that they are Light workers. They radiate a powerful positive energy around people they attract, those unfortunate people who are empty or have a problem in life. Without realising it, they radiate a type of happy glow and a special presence when they meet people for the first time.

All the Light workers I have met share a very common trait. They don't feel as if they "belong". They can find fitting into groups of people, including groups of friends or groups at school, very difficult. They look at everything differently and think "outside of the box". Often ridiculed in groups with expressions like, "What planet do you come from?" and accused of being over-emotional or lacking in logic, the reality is that they are truly different. Very often they are misunderstood and not accepted for what they are. They are simply not like everyone else.

Part of the reason is that many people are caught up in a world of negativity and subconsciously sense that the Light worker can see right through them. Without even understanding it, the Light worker may be sending out vibes of healing and peace. And this can "throw" the other person to react badly towards them, because they don't understand why this person is having this effect. Their individuality stands out. Their happy-go-lucky spirit can irritate people, can cause confusion and fear. So many Light workers find they have to put on a "front" and develop a personality so that they can fit in. They are afraid to be themselves and this can be disastrous. It is far better that they pluck up the confidence to be their real selves. But this can take years.

Very often they find it hard to make friends and this poses big problems later on when developing relationships in love. It's only when they become enlightened as to their own special powers that they break free from this prison. Then they fully develop and become the natural beacons of light that will bring the kind of spirituality to the world that they were meant to in the first place. But they need to break free, and be honest with themselves.

Most of them, however, are naturally very gifted and special people. They are unselfish and have very little respect for material things. Many of those I know give away a lot of personal belongings easily. Their generosity, in the wrong hands, can be taken advantage of. They are not great with money and don't value it, which is why many of them can get into financial difficulties. Many of them are constantly being told that they are useless with money! As for ego – they don't possess it. While they may appear outwardly confident, this should never be confused with ego. Ego is not love. So they are not egotists.

One of the key things about them is that they have the ability to gain a "spiritual awakening" much faster than other people. They can sometimes be accused of being "dreamers", and maybe they are. But it's because of their spiritual connection, which may be dormant and not obvious to them, that they feel an innate ability to evaluate everything on a "hunch" or a "gut feeling". Many of them don't seem to realise that their abilities are coming from God, a higher power, and that takes time to fully understand. They have to work on it.

Very often, I see people from all professions making huge career changes suddenly and unexpectedly. This tends to happen once they realise how important their spiritual connection actually is. It's then that they opt to work with healings or counselling work of some kind. Once they finally realise their real role in life and begin to work on their natural talents, they will find it very hard at first. Because only then will they decide that they have to give up certain things, including a reliance on materialist things. It's only then that they will release their minds and take up the mission on Earth for which they were sent in the first place. And then they will hone their skills and finally feel comfortable in themselves, probably for the first time in their life.

Many of them have premonitions, make quick decisions based on gut feeling. Some even have mystical experiences. They develop powerful healing abilities which were untapped up to now. Some will focus on religion; many will say that religion has nothing to do with it. But there is a connection with the maker of all things, with God. Jesus, for example, was a mystic and the most powerful healer that ever walked the Earth. So straight away there is a connection with God. And while some religions tell you not to meditate, meditation is part and parcel of what Light workers need to do to keep in touch with their spirituality.

Our Lady tells me, for example, to meditate on the Rosary, to "feel the pain that my Son went through on Earth". She has often asked me to meditate on the sorrow and the suffering of all God's children on Earth. It is only by connection with the higher consciousness that is God that Light workers finally understand fully what their role on Earth is all about. The Light workers on Earth today are about to herald a new dawning – a new age, a new Light. God's Light. To help people to flourish, find love and joy, not only on Earth but in their spiritual futures.

Victim Soul

11

Torment by Satan Begins

At first I wasn't sure whether it was my imagination. Was it a direct result of the stress of the apparitions and the harassment my family and I were going through from the media? But soon one thing was clear to me: the number of times I saw, heard and felt Satan, not only in my dreams, but during the day and at night, began to increase, and with greater intensity right after the apparition at Knock on October 31st 2009. The horrific physical and mental abuse and sheer torment that I endured are distasteful, sickening and too shocking to recount fully or in any great detail.

During my trips to Knock, I have met many wonderful people – those with a strong, deep faith, including lay people, young and old, as well as representatives from various religious orders. One of the first pieces of advice given to me by a wonderful nun, as soon as she realised that I was a genuine visionary, was to "seek protection".

"Joe, you must seek protection. You are now a target. Don't you know?" she whispered to me gently.

She explained to me that, in the past, other visionaries and mystics, including Sr Faustina and Padre Pio, suffered a similar fate, where they would be attacked by Satan both mentally and physically. In addition, she explained that many devout Christians, in Ireland and around the world, have reported satanic attacks. I was assured that I was not alone. She told me that it was an ordeal I would have to accept as part of my work, as part and parcel of the gift I have been given. I should offer this suffering up to save souls.

Face-to-face Attacks

My experiences, where Satan attacks me face-to-face, have presented bigger challenges than I have had to face during exorcisms. At times, they have nearly broken me. Yet somehow I always seem to bounce back. Fight back. Occurring at least twice a week, they get worse the more messages I receive from Our Lady. I know with certainty now that the stronger my connection with Our Lady becomes the more Satan tries to attack me. The attacks have increased during the writing of this book and become more ferocious, more vicious.

As already stated in this book, Satan's single biggest talent is to convince people that he doesn't exist. So when the attacks come, it is very hard indeed to explain to other people what's happening.

Just to reassure those of you who are now saying, "But why would anyone want to start praying, knowing all this? Who, in their right mind would want to develop their religion at all?", rarely does Satan attack those who are not posing an immediate threat to him and his evil ways. He only targets those who are close and working directly on behalf of God to bring about change of some kind.

He attacks in a number of ways. To start with, he will cause complete havoc around you. His favourite trick is to engineer arguments and rifts between you and your friends, colleagues and family. This is done to challenge you first in the hope of provoking the desired reaction – i.e. they will wear you down and you will give up what you are doing in God's name to deal with these disruptive issues. These types of attack are particularly hurtful because they affect your personal life and the close relationships you enjoy. They happen so suddenly they take you by complete surprise.

While he's at it, he immediately sets out to create other unexpected problems in your life – usually relating to loss of income or lack of money. Very often, these can involve legal problems that just don't make sense – they arise literally out of the blue! What on Earth is going on? Then, before you can answer this question, people – strangers – will enter your life suddenly, bearing bad news.

Obstacles designed to disrupt your relationship with God crop up when you least expect them. For example, on my way into the church, I would get a call from someone to distract me, usually to prevent me entering the house of God. Or during the course of this book – and my co-writer will vouch for this – computers have turned off unexpectedly every time we wrote the piece about Satan together. Lights would switch off in the room. Electric power would fail. Internet access would cease without explanation, right when she would be emailing the next section of the book draft for editing. Phone lines would die. Content, already written and contained in computer files, would go missing, despite having been saved in a folder beforehand. I could go on.

Not long after the apparitions in October 2009, I was forced to close down my beloved prayer room in my local area of Ballyfermot, my little haven of peace and love, where I helped heal so many wonderful people both on a spiritual level and from terminal illnesses. But I regretted its closure for another reason. Satan never attacked me there. Even during my daily prayers (he loves to attack just before you start to pray), he never managed to attack. So I always felt safe there, as the room was completely protected and blessed.

Immediately after that, the more serious satanic attacks began in earnest – in my home, during the day while at prayer, and at night. I tried to hide what was happening from my family, but it was impossible to do that so I tried to play it down as best I could. I did, however, share everything with Seán, my eldest son, who has witnessed some frightening events at home.

The first serious attack occurred one night, as I lay twisting and turning, trying to get to sleep. I felt him, Satan, the Evil One, lurking in my room. His long cold slimy hands curled their way around my throat, sharp claws dug deep into my flesh and squeezed slowly and deliberately until I couldn't breathe. Gagging, panicking, I felt my lungs bursting. The stench from his breath nearly knocked me out. I managed to stay conscious. His hold eased slightly. Before I could draw my first deep breath, an incredible force suddenly yanked the rosary beads and cross from around my neck. My head pulled back now, I was dragged out of the bed. I was flung to the floor, face down. He threw himself on top of me, clawing at my back, punching me hard into every soft part of my back and my buttocks. Then, turning me over, he punched me in the stomach, my chest, my neck, my face – I was now being pummelled by an army of demons in every part of my body as he screamed obscenities.

Weak now, with the sweat dripping from every pore in my body, I looked right into the face of the beast from Hell! I was immediately struck by what at first seemed to be a surprisingly handsome face. But it was an evil and angry face, and with its manic grin and evil eyes. I thought I would vomit from the disgust I felt. It is a face no one on this Earth should ever have to look at. But look at him I did – defiantly, with a courage I didn't feel – straight into those black gleaming eyes filled with absolute hatred. I thought he would kill me then. Almost senseless by now and terrified out of my wits, I called on the Archangel St Michael to help me, using my favourite prayer to him:

> *Saint Michael the Archangel, defend us in battle. Be our protection against the wickedness and snares of the Devil. May God rebuke him, we humbly pray; and do Thou, O Prince of the Heavenly Host – by the Divine Power of God – cast into Hell Satan and all the evil spirits, who roam throughout the world seeking the ruin of souls. Amen.*

Lying in agony, writhing on the floor, I looked up then at the scene which, in slow motion, rolled out before me. I could see the Archangel Michael stand guard over me, sword in hand, telling Satan that he wouldn't win. Satan by now was cowering in fear.

Then, just as soon as it all began, the vision disappeared and the room was now in complete silence. Tranquillity returned and I slept through the night without any further disruption.

The following morning, I woke up covered in marks, long vicious red scars like nail-scratches and deep purple bruises on my neck, my back, my legs and my stomach. These marks which appear the next morning have become a regular feature of these attacks. Sometimes it is only when I get into the shower that they come up. They are not open wounds however. My body was still throbbing with the pain. It's only then that the reality of it all came rushing back. I could still smell the fear from the night before and the panic set in. *When is this going to stop?* I asked myself.

Inspection by an Exorcist

In November 2009, I met with priest who had worked for years as an exorcist. After our discussion he declared me to be an authentic visionary, seer and mystic.

"You know, Joe," he said to me gently, "you may not realise it, but you are a very powerful man. A holy man. You do Our Lady's work very well. It is very hard work. You should know, Joe, however, that as part of your work for Our Blessed Mother, you are going to be hurt. You'll suffer. You will be ridiculed. Laughed at. Belittled. Mocked. You are going to find it very difficult to stand up and tell the world what you know. It will be anything but easy. Because you work from your heart and when you work from your heart you are working with pure love. The love of God."

As he put his hand on my head and blessed me, I

burst into tears. I could feel an immense sense of love from God coming through, like a pure channel, from this man's heart right into the core of my own heart. I was filled with the most beautiful, unconditional love. He told me he felt that I should be treated as an authentic mystic for our Blessed Mother. He also told me I was a messenger for God and that I was chosen for this work deliberately.

It was just then that he revealed to me that I was a victim soul, a term I had never heard before. "A victim soul? What's that, Father?" I asked. He told me that when a person is chosen to work on behalf of God, he or she can unfortunately expect the suffering that goes with it. They will, he told me, suffer more than most people during life. It is important, however, that they offer up their suffering in union with Jesus, as an example of Christ's own Passion and Death. The motive of a victim soul is to show great love of God and desire to help redeem people's souls.

After about fifteen minutes, the priest asked me to sit in the chair opposite him. During this period he told me he had the gift to look into people's souls and that he had not only looked into mine but that he had confessed me and that I was now infused with the love of the Holy Spirit.

He asked me to tell him about myself. I told him about my visit to Medjugorje and the fact that Our Lady asked me to go to Knock to reveal her messages. He replied, "This is now part of your journey in this world. It's a ministry. I have cleansed you today. I can see that you have the power to rid people of demons. You have exorcised people, Joe, haven't you? I know that you have done this. You've helped rescue souls to move into the Light too, haven't you?"

"I have, Father. I have been doing this all my life," I told him.

"You are not to worry, Joe," he continued, "because, despite the dangers you see around you, you are very much protected. You are in the spirit world and you have been blessed."

He then told me that, as a victim soul, I would have to endure a lot of torment in my life. He went on to say, "God rejoices in the work that you do. But you are going to be knocked. Yet you have so much faith. And you will stay strong."

Then he handed me a beautiful Benedictine Cross as a gift. He urged me to wear it, along with a vial of special holy oil that he himself used in exorcisms.

The Benedictine Cross is actually a medal, on one side of which is a cross. Saint Benedict had a great devotion to the Cross of Jesus and faith in its power. He worked many miracles using the Sign of the Cross and used it to dispel evil and exorcise demons. The Benedictine Cross symbolises this by the inscriptions on the medal. It is still the most common instrument used by exorcists to set victims of demons free. On the medal is an image of St Benedict, holding a cross and the Holy Rule of his order. On the one side of his figure is a cup, on the other a raven. The cup is the poisoned cup enemies offered to him, which shattered when he made the Sign of the Cross over it. The raven is about to carry away a loaf of poisoned bread a jealous enemy had sent to Benedict. The reverse of the medal has a cross with the initial letters of the words, *Non Draco Sit Mihi Dux* ("Let not the dragon be my guide"), on its horizontal bar. Round the margin stand the initial letters of the words *Vade Retro Satana, Nunquam Suade Mihi Vana – Sunt Mala Quae Libas, Ipse Venena Bibas* ("Go behind, Satan, do not suggest to me your vanities – Evil are the things you offer, drink your own poison").

One last word of warning the priest gave me was this: when you become so close to Our Lady and the Blessed Trinity, the Devil will torment you. And because of the role Our Lady plays as his greatest adversary (a gift given to her by God), anyone who works actively for her, whether they are visionaries or mystics, will be targeted by the Evil One. He seeks out these people above anyone else because of their power and the links they have to her.

"You will have to learn to fight him, Joe, and you will need to know how. Angels have been assigned to you to keep you protected at all times."

Finally he told me to be careful about how I publish the messages I receive from Our Lady, as they are sacred. In the wrong hands, he explained, they would be twisted and would become the subject of public ridicule. He also explained to me that I would need to find a spiritual director – a priest experienced in such matters who would be able to guide me in my work. He explained that often visionaries need assistance as they receive messages but often don't realise the significance of them. Bernadette of Lourdes had one, he told me, as do the visionaries of Medjugorje. As someone who is fairly ignorant when it comes to understanding prayer, aspects of the Bible and other ways of praying, I told him that I would welcome such a person. He doubted that I would find such a priest immediately, because spiritual directors need to be strong enough – especially in their understanding of Satan. As we parted, he said, "Our Lady will eventually get you one."

Just after the New Year, as work began on this book, the attacks began to get worse. As I got back into the daily routine of saying the Holy Rosary and preparing for the next apparition (which I did not make public), the attacks intensified. I tried to get a spiritual director as the exorcist had advised but to no avail. No priest I found had the experience or knowledge I needed in my situation.

The nights especially became more terrifying, although I did also have day-time experiences. As I would be getting ready for bed, the air would become freezing. Almost in a split second, the coldness would wind its way around my body, but wouldn't be felt anywhere else in the room. Then the smell – like sulphur or the rotting body of a large animal – would release itself slowly around the room. That's when I would brace myself for what was to come.

First the vicious deep growling voice: "I'll f****** stop you with your messages!" he would scream in my ear. Then the blasphemy when he would call Our Lady, God the Father and Jesus Christ the most barbaric names imaginable, terms which I would never repeat.

His tone would change when he would try to entice me with promises. "Come work with me, Joe. Your life will be much easier. I'll give you anything you desire. Money. Power. Just name it. It's all yours. I have huge powers."

Although afraid, I would never let him see my fear "Go away! There's no power greater than God. I am one in God, there is no separation." This last phrase is the one I use every day for protection. I then make the Sign of the Cross and say, "I burn you out in the name of Jesus Christ."

Eventually he would go away. But the terror didn't. These attacks are much more frightening than the exorcisms which I attend, because it is during these particular attacks that I know he tries to kill me. But he can't; Our Lady has told me he won't be able to because of the protection she has instilled around me.

12

The Core Message, Early 2010

During January and February 2010, the messages from Our Lady became more frequent and more urgent. While similar to previous ones, they were very specific. For the most part they urged people to pray and to convert to believing in God again, to counteract evil in the world. But since December 2009, they referred, in particular, to the "lack of time" there is in the world for people to convert and believe in God again. In one of the messages which have not been made public before this, Our Lady revealed that Jesus Christ will make himself known when he returns to Earth and it will be very soon, in events which will be witnessed the world over. I believe that it is a matter of years not decades. When Our Lady refers to time she makes it clear that the Second Coming is very soon. Her messages during this time emphasised the importance of people reciting the Holy Rosary at a time of great turmoil and hardship in the world so that souls, other than those saying the Rosary, "can be saved".

So who is Our Lady communicating with? Is it the Catholic population? This is a question I have asked her, because it worried me. And she made this very clear to me: she told me that she is, as a messenger of God, reaching out to all people on Earth. It does not matter what creed you follow. Everyone, including non-believers, are all God's children. There is only one eternal God, she says, the Creator of all things past, present and to come. She claims there is only one religion – and that is belief in one God. The God referred to in the Holy Bible – her "Father's Book" as she refers to it.

She is trying to communicate with all people, all religions. Her messages are for everyone. It is more about people's faith. She has explained to me that Jesus did not die just for people of the Catholic faith; he died for all the sins of the world and for every soul born with original sin. She is imploring God's children around the world, of all creeds, colours and races, to convert back to God and a spiritual life, to the one true God, the God referred to in the Holy Bible – the one true God she speaks of. When she speaks to me, she asks me to get people to say her "most Holy Rosary", because it has so much power when prayed from the heart. I realise that many religions don't say the Rosary but this is the message I am getting so I simply impart it. Of course it was renowned as a Christian prayer going way back to the ninth century and there is a Protestant version of it too! There is no problem, no obstacle, no heartache, no matter how hard, that can't be overcome or resolved by praying the Holy Rosary, as she keeps telling me. The Rosary offers huge protection for everyone and she urges people to learn how to say it. (A full description of how to pray the Rosary is included in the final chapters of this book.) A real mystery in itself, there were only three sets of Mysteries known for almost eight hundred years: the Joyful, the Sorrowful and the Glorious Mysteries. The last set of mysteries, "The Mysteries of Light", was introduced by the late Pope John Paul II. Our Lady says that today only four out of five are known. One more set of mysteries has still to be revealed before we know the full extent of what the Rosary code means.

She keeps referring to the "Prince of Darkness" (meaning Satan); he cries and melts, she says, when the Holy Rosary is said from the heart. It is the story of Our Lord Jesus Christ – His birth, His life on Earth, His suffering, His death, His resurrection and His ascension into Heaven. Very few people are clear as to the full mystery and power associated with the Rosary. One thing is abundantly clear, though. People who say the Rosary will merit a high degree of glory in Heaven, according to Our Lady.

During this period, early 2010, I was working with RTÉ, the Irish national television channel, on a documentary about the Knock apparitions. The filming could be very hard work at times, harder still when I had a daily routine that involved devotion to Our Blessed Mother.

During this time, I received stronger messages than ever.

Here follows an account of the messages.

Message received, Saturday, February 13th 2010 (3.15 p.m.), in my house.

Brief reference to the Second Coming and the Rise of the Antichrist.

"My dear child, cease worrying, for it is a negative emotion. Trust more in your Father.

"I know it has been very difficult for you for the past number of months. I am never away from you. I am with you, with your work.

"Some things I must share with you today regarding the return on Earth of my beloved Son, Jesus the Christ. The church is starting to listen to my messages. This is good news. You must tell my children I am happy with them.

"They must pray more every day for conversion for all of God's children everywhere. Pray for the lost souls, that they may be redeemed from purgatory. Pray my most Holy Rosary so that the Antichrist

will not win over my children. For he, the Deceiver, is here on Earth. He is very powerful, very dangerous, very cunning, very charming, very deceitful. He is in my Father's House on Earth. My priests, bishops and cardinals are infested with his ill-gotten ways and his power.

"The world, my child, is ripe now for he who waits in darkness to make himself known to mankind. Pray, pray, pray. Never stop praying. For by praying the most Holy Rosary, the evil one can be kept at bay. I am always watching over you, my child, please don't worry. For everything is written in my Father's Book. Thank you for responding to my call.

"Mother of Love and Peace."

Message received, Sunday, February 14th 2010 (10.45 p.m.), in my house

Referring to turmoil in Ireland and around the world and the persecution of the Catholic Church by Satan and his army.

"Good evening, my child. Thank you for responding to my call.

"Tonight I fill you with words of wisdom. For the truth will be known, my child, through you. I have

informed my angels to protect you with your channel. The church is going through a great persecution at this time. Pray, pray, pray my most Holy Rosary, for this is one way of lifting the persecution from my priests, my bishops and my cardinals and most of all from all of my children from all over the world. Satan is trying to destroy as many souls as he can. In this time of great recession in the world, especially in Ireland, he has got into so many young people, turning them towards darkness, drugs, sins of the flesh, robbery of their neighbours, material things such as money and greed. Be very careful, for the Deceiver is prowling, just waiting to devour. Pray every day. Call your angels and they will help you. Pray to my beloved Son, Jesus the Christ.

[pause]

"Joe, this is the prayer you must say every day for protection against the evil one and to help the souls in purgatory: 'O Jesus, forgive us our sins. Save us from the fires of Hell. Lead all souls to Heaven, especially those in most need of Thy mercy.'

"Say this prayer three times every day. It has great power against the evil one. Rest now, my child, you are covered in my most powerful and most holy mantle. Thank you.

"Mother of Peace and Mercy. Amen."

Message received, Monday, February 15th 2010 (11.45 a.m.) in my house

Predicting Next Apparition for February 22nd 2010

"My dear child, I am your Blessed Mother. I am very happy with your response to my call. You are doing quite well now. You have opened up much stronger to receiving my message. Peace be with you.

"When God, our eternal Father, made the world out of nothing He made Adam and Eve. God's commandments have been mocked and broken by the ones He has created. Satan has made this happen. He, the Deceiver, must be stopped now before it is too late.

"My child, time is running out. People must go back to God and obey His commandments. It is good that you have been praying for our priests and our church and the lost souls in purgatory. Prayers are always answered when prayed from the heart.

"You, my dear child, must not knock yourself for your mistakes. You must praise God for your faith with your work. My child, you will experience me much more differently at Knock on 22 February. This will be a huge apparition,

for you and the world. For it is written in my Father's Book that you must keep praying. Pray my most Holy Rosary every day. Receive my Son at Holy Mass, go to Confession.

"You have been chosen and been given many graces. You, my child, have been guided by all of God's angels. Peace and love and prayer be with you always. Remember, the power of love through prayer has the strength to move mountains and also to keep the Deceiver at bay.

"Bless you, my child. Heaven rejoices in your faith. Go now in peace and love and joy; in my Father's Holy Name I bless you, the Father, the Son and the most Holy Spirit. Thank you for responding to my call.

"Mother of peace and joy and love, Mother of Jesus, the Christ, Mother Mary, Queen of Peace."

Message received through apparition, Tuesday, February 16th 2010 (2.30–4 p.m.), St Matthew's Church, Ballyfermot (during live filming of TV documentary)

These events took place in the local church but were not predicted in advance.

First vision 2.30 p.m.
Message indicating that the Antichrist is in the Vatican

I was sitting in the church during filming, when suddenly I looked up at the statue of the Blessed Virgin, because I felt the tears coming – always a sign that Our Lady is about to appear. I saw her manifest herself to the side of the statue, and then she was smiling at me gently. She spoke as follows:

> *"Welcome, my dear child. It's okay, everything is written in my Father's Book. Relax, my sweet one. I am preparing you for later on. Accept my graces. Today, my sweet child, I will speak with you at 3 p.m. Your heart is open now, my child. Everything is as it should be."*

Then she turned her head around and vanished. All I could see was the statue.

Second vision, 3 p.m.
Message stating that Jesus is here on Earth now

I was looking at the statue of the Mother and Child when I saw a white mist form around it. Our Lady called to me and said, *"Come forth, my child, do not be afraid. I am your Blessed Mother."*

I got off the seat and walked up to the statue, lit a candle, knelt down on the floor and looked at the face of the Mother in the statue. It then began to change into Jesus. Looking at Him, my heart swelled with love. He had brown shoulder-length hair, a short beard and piercing blue eyes with sallow skin – a very striking, incredibly handsome man. Then, suddenly, the image turned into the famous Saint Padre Pio. Finally the image turned back into Our Blessed Mother. My eyes were drawn to the Infant Jesus, whom she was now holding in her arms. I looked closer and then he turned into the most beautiful white lamb. On the throat of the lamb there was some red blood. I was filled with love and compassion. By now, I was looking at Our Lady in full physical form. She was wearing a long white gown with flowers around her feet – floating above the ground. At this stage, the Lamb of God had gone and the statue on the altar had gone. All I could see was her. I said to Mother, "Why are you showing me this? I don't understand." She held her hands out to me as if she was going to embrace me and said:

> *"My dear child, this is the Lamb of God who takes away the sins of the world. Tell my children to come back to my Son. Time is near, very near. They must listen to my message. They must obey our Eternal Father's commandments. My Son Jesus is on the Earth. He walks in Egypt. The Catholic Church needs much prayer. Ireland needs help with conversion and prayer. The*

Antichrist is prowling with his army of deceivers. He is everywhere. He is in my Father's House in Rome and all over the world. He must be stopped now. Pray, pray, pray. Tell my children that when they pray my most Holy Rosary, they are bringing light back to the Earth. For Light is healing. Light is conversion. Light is God. I implore you, my child, to gather my flock together at Knock. Multitudes will gather soon through my message and you, my child, will lead them.

"For you have been chosen. You are ready now. You are strong. The time is right now. My people will listen to you. Do not be afraid; I am with you always. You are never alone, my sweet child. For you have also chosen this work. You must not listen to unclean spirits. For they are here to try to stop our work, God's work. It is a battle we must win, my child. And the light will triumph in the end.

"Pray for Pope Benedict, for he is under great attack at this moment in time. They will try to dethrone him from his seat of justice. Go now, my shepherd. Gather my flock and teach them to love thy God. Praise God every day. Go with light and love. Go in God's Most Holy Name. Never cease loving God, for you, my dear child, are part of God's creation. Thank you for

responding to my call. Rest now, my precious child.

"Mary, Mother of Peace and Love."

No sooner had I sat down again in the church than she showed me visions of Hell. I will never forget it. It was extremely disturbing; terrifying, in fact. It looked like a massive, never-ending, wide black river, almost like a lake, with flames of fire shooting off the surface. Only two colours were visible to me, black and red. I could see clearly that the poor unfortunate souls there never get a break from screaming and torture, or release of any kind. As soon as they would surface, they would appear to me first as ordinary people, including children (which really threw me) and then they would turn into the most ugly creatures imaginable. They screamed, roared, cried, squirmed in terrible pain. It was extremely upsetting. I felt ill when I saw this image.

And then I was shown the souls crying and pleading for mercy in purgatory. I had never been too sure about the existence of purgatory – now I knew that this was a mistake. Yes, sadly it really does exist. But these souls can be saved. They simply need prayer, and lots of it.

It was then that Our Lady showed me a calendar with the date clearly shown. It was July 10th 2015. She told me, "This is the last chance for conversion. The last chance for redemption. The world is in turmoil; disasters are everywhere. I promise my special protection and the greatest graces to all those who recite the Rosary."

Message received, Thursday, 18th February, 3 p.m. at home
(recited live over the phone during interview for this book, while in channel)

On the Rosary

Referring to the Holy Rosary, Mother's message is as follows:

> *"Pray the Holy Rosary. It will cause virtue and good works to flourish. It will obtain for souls the abundant mercy of God. It will withdraw the hearts of men from the love of the world and its vanities. It will lift them to a desire of eternal things. Oh, that souls will sanctify themselves by this means! The soul which recommends itself to me by the recitation of the Rosary shall not perish.*
>
> *"Whoever shall have a true devotion to the Rosary shall not die without the sacrament of the Church. Those who are faithful to the recitation of the Holy Rosary shall have, during their life on Earth, the light of God and the plenitude of graces. At the moment of death they*

shall participate in the merit of the saints in paradise. I shall deliver from purgatory those who have been devoted to my Rosary. I have obtained from my Divine Son that all my advocates of the Rosary shall have for intercessors the entire Celestial Court during their life and at the hour of death. All those who recite the Rosary are my sons and brothers of my Son Jesus Christ. The devotion to my most Holy Rosary is a great sign of pre-destination.

Urgency of Messages Increase

After that I realised that her messages were getting more urgent. I know now that something important is going to happen on Earth. She has told me that all her Churches on Earth will amalgamate as one Church and will adore the one God.

She mentions the words "false prophets" a lot, as Jesus did in his time on Earth. "Be wary of the false prophets because they are working for the Deceiver to undermine the truth."

"What type of prophets?" I asked her.

She explained that it concerned those preaching beliefs, including religion, about different Gods, different concepts. Then she warned about idolatry, that is, adoring other human beings and placing them on a pedestal or giving people, objects, material things precedence in your life above all else including loved ones.

Message received in Knock, Monday, February 22nd 2010
Urging the Catholic Church to listen.

There were over fifty people in the church already, praying the Rosary, when I arrived. The documentary camera crew was in the church. To avoid distraction, I asked them not to point the camera in front of my face but to keep it to one side. The last thing I needed was a distraction on that day of all days. At previous apparitions, including the one on October 31st and the following one on December 5th, I had found the cameras to be very intrusive.

As the Rosary was coming to an end, I could feel a powerful heat on my back. Yes, the sun was shining in that part of the church, but this was stronger than that.

While kneeling reciting the Rosary, I began to stare up at the coloured glass pane in the window above the altar. I immediately felt the presence of our Blessed Mother coming to me. Then I could hear her saying to me, "Welcome, my child. Do not be afraid. I am your Blessed Mother."

I got up from my seat and stood in front of the altar. As I looked up at the window, located high up right behind the altar, it appeared to smash into millions of tiny fragments which then turned into tiny sparkles of white light, all of them circling and illuminating the window.

Our Blessed Mother appeared in full splendour. She was smiling. Her cloak was sky-blue and her gown gleaming white. That day she wore a gold crown with red jewels that glittered. Her bare feet were covered with red roses.

Suddenly the window began to take the form of a grotto. Our Lady was surrounded by an amazing cloud of brilliant white haze with a gentle mist. I could see her heart. It was bleeding red blood, but not a lot. She did not seem to be in any pain. She was smiling as she stretched out both her arms towards me. The most incredible pink light shone out from her hands. Above her I could see Jesus Christ standing, looking down. I felt weak at that stage, my heart saturated with pure white love.

Then I could see Padre Pio to the left side of Jesus. It was then that I was really taken by surprise, as I could see the late Pope John Paul II to the right of Our Lady.

With that, the lamb on the altar below Our Lady turned to gold as a drop of blood from her heart fell onto the lamb's back. The angels which feature on the actual wall of the church then turned gold and I heard Our Lady say, *"Thank you for coming today, my sweet child. Kneel now, my child, and receive my grace."*

I knelt down and she filled me with the most beautiful lights and love. This is the message she gave me on that day.

> *"I am happy today, my children are praying. Thank my people for praying and singing my praise. I am happy for all who come today. Peace be with you. All my Father's priests,*

bishops, cardinals must come together. They must listen to my seers. They must heed my messages. They must respond to my Father's call for conversion and unity among all nations. They are not responding the way God wants them to. They know the way and how to respond. My heart bleeds for my Church. My Church must be respected. But respect must also come from my Church. The foundations have been rocked and will continue to be rocked until the truth is known. Satan, the Deceiver, is responsible for this turn-around. He is among my Church. He must be stopped now, before it is too late, as time is running out.

"My Son desires to make himself known soon, here on Earth. He will walk again. The return of Our Saviour will not, and must not, and cannot be prevented. For it is written in my Father's Book. Pray, pray, pray, my child, every day for conversion. Pray for the lost souls. We must not allow Satan to take them. Satan cannot, and must not, win. Pray for peace among my church leaders.

"There are great changes ahead, my child. For the love of God, tell them to confess and pray to my Son Jesus, the Christ. They must learn to pray from their hearts. They must show grace and peace and love and kindness to all peoples of

the world. The doors must not be closed, they must be opened to all who come in the name of God. The Antichrist laughs when my priests do not listen to my seers. My child, a great darkness is descending over my church, all over the globe. My Father's commandments must be respected.

"My dear child, tell my priests that if they do not heed my messages, they will be taken out of their authority. They must be exposed now before they can do more damage to my Church. My beloved children must be protected at all times. My beloved workers, my visionaries, my seers throughout the world must be given recognition by the Church. They must be respected and listened to, for they were given many graces and many gifts from the Holy Spirit to do their work for God, the eternal Father. Soon my beloved seers, my messengers, my visionaries, my healers will be brought together. My Light workers will all merge as one in the battle against the Deceiver. Rome must welcome them with open arms. This, my dear child, will happen soon.

"Rejection against my seers is a sin against God. The Church on Earth fears losing its power to my messengers of light. Rest now, my child, you have done well today. My angels are protecting you, have no fear. Remember, the Church will

listen to all my seers, my visionaries and my Light workers.

"Enough for now. Thank you for responding today. Go now in peace and love.

"Mother of Peace and Joy. Mary, Mother of Jesus."

The Sun Begins to Spin again

As I walked out of the church that day, I noticed people gathering to look up at the sun which, yet again, began to spin in the sky. Seemingly, when I was in the church during the apparition, it had come out from behind the clouds with a dull silver disc covering it, reducing the glare. It then moved out of the clouds completely and for a full fifty minutes, according to one witnes, Caroline Brady, who stood awestruck the entire time and timed it – all in the presence of an RTÉ crew – we all watched it dance, spin, get smaller and then larger with a mesh-like disc covering it. There were no clouds in sight. It dazzled, rocked from side to side, the ring around it shook and then lots of colours appeared to glow around the circumference. Other witnesses there, many of whom had seen the previous events in Knock during October 2009, claim that this was the strongest one they had seen to date since the apparition on October 31st 2009. For the others who had not been there, it was the most incredible sight they have ever seen. A miracle. There's no other word for it as many claimed on the day.

Message received, Thursday, February 25th 2010, at home

Three days later I received another message from Our Lady. This time it was mid-morning in my home as I went into channel.

> *"Hello, my dear child. Some words for today. I want to thank you for responding to my call. You, my child, are beginning to comprehend my messages. I will also be protecting you, my sweet child. You make me so happy when you come before me at Knock. I know it is very difficult and hard for you at times. I always ease your burden. If you could see yourself when praying, you would see all your angels around you. So pure you are, my dear child. You must pray for non-believers. You must pray for their souls.*
>
> *"Sin is spreading like wildfire. It will destroy my children unless people continue to pray my most Holy Rosary every day for non-believers.*
>
> *"Knock will bring multitudes through you, my child. Conversion will happen.*

"You are strong now. Stronger than ever before. You are very much loved and protected by all of God's angels. You, my sweet dear child, my chosen one, take all of this work for granted and you are right. All that has been given to you is granted. You are so positive, my child, you let nothing hinder you, for your faith and belief have multiplied a thousand times since your return from Medjugorje. Everything you do, my child, you offer up to my beloved Son, Jesus the Christ. Rest now, my child. There is much more work you must do. Everything is being taken care of. Journey well, my dear sweet child of God.

"Peace and love be with you.

"Your loving Blessed Mother of Jesus the Christ, Mother of Compassion and Love."

Most Difficult Apparition of All

March 10th 2010

13

Death of a Fellow Visionary

My heart was broken when, on March 3rd 2010, one of my best friends was killed, only hours after his first child was born. Keith Henderson, as mentioned earlier in this book, was my fellow visionary and I loved him like a brother. He attended all the apparitions with me up to and including the one on January 11th 2010. His love and devotion to Our Blessed Mother was absolute.

Even though I know now, with total conviction, that he is at peace in Heaven, at the time I was completely devastated and inconsolable. I just couldn't make sense of it all. Why did he die? Why then, just as our work for Our Lady on Earth was intensifying? I couldn't come to terms with any of it. Bewildered, saddened, and unable to make sense of it all, I asked Jesus, why? Why did this holy man have to go? All I could think of was his poor wife and baby son. How could this happen?

I was in a complete daze. I couldn't even talk to

Our Lady. I found it hard to go into channel. I couldn't sleep, couldn't concentrate. The memories kept flooding back. I thought of the deep love that Keith had for Our Lady; the work she wanted us to carry out for her; the beautiful devotion he had for Jesus Christ. I remembered all the times he sat on his own in the church, on Sunday afternoons, at the Eucharistic adoration. He would sit before the altar, remain silent and pray for hours. Then the thoughts of his precious new baby would come back again to haunt me and I prayed constantly for his wife to be given the strength she needed at this terrible time.

These images kept dancing around in my head, every minute of the day. Never would I forget Keith's gentleness, the love in his eyes, his goodness and his steely determination to do good work on this Earth to save souls. Love was at the core of his very essence. I will never ever forget him as long as I live.

Today I know he is watching over me and I know he is in the Light and in Heaven. He will work with me, in Heaven, to help lost souls on this Earth to seek redemption. That was our goal. That is still our goal. And it will be forever.

Interruption of the Holy Rosary in Knock

Difficult though it was, I knew that I had to fulfil the promise to Our Lady and travel to Knock for the next apparition only one week later. So, on the morning of March 10th 2010, I got a lift from a friend to Knock, taking with me a beautiful photo of Keith, which I had taken of him in front of a statue of Our Lady in my prayer room some time before. I'd had it enlarged, mounted and framed specially, as I wanted to place it on the altar in the Apparition Chapel on that special day.

The only people who were aware of the predicted apparition were the editors of this book, RTÉ's documentary crew (who were travelling that day to film); the people at the Knock Shrine who had to be informed because of the TV crew, and two friends. Since the end of 2009, I had decided I just couldn't face the barrage of abuse from the media and members of the public. It was just too difficult, not only on me, but on my family. Yet I knew in my heart that everyone had the right to know what was happening. But how to get these messages out was another challenge, and one I would have to face soon. I had heard through the grapevine, though, that a number of prayer-group members from around the country would be going along that day.

It was a glorious sunny day. On arriving at the Knock Shrine, I went into the Old Parish Church to say a brief prayer and saw a notice announcing that the daily Mass would take place at three o'clock there. As I was going into the other chapel to say the Rosary, I felt sad that so few people knew what was going on.

Imagine, they had no idea that an apparition of the Blessed Virgin Mary was about to happen behind that church in less than an hour. Walking around to the side, and then behind the old church, I approached the Apparition Chapel, a small, separate chapel, as I described before, tucked right behind the old church. To my delight, I was met by a number of people – well-wishers and a small number of those who had attended previous apparitions. Some of them had brought friends who had come to see the apparition for themselves. Yes, word of mouth is a great way of spreading news. One person I had told at the last apparition had got the word out, without the media finding out. These people were not what you would call "sensation seekers". No, they were a mix of spiritual people, genuine Christian believers, Catholics, non-believers, all looking for an answer. Some of them were local people. Others came from surrounding counties, including County Mayo itself, Galway, Longford, Donegal and as far away as Dublin. Each of them in turn introduced themselves to me just as I headed towards the confessional centre.

After receiving absolution at confession, from the local priest at Knock, as Our Lady told me I must do before any apparition, I walked into the Apparition Chapel at 2.50 p.m. I noticed, but didn't pay much attention at the time to a red security van, with a security guard and a representative from Knock Shrine standing beside it. I looked over, caught his eye and nodded. He didn't. Neither of them responded. They looked away. This didn't surprise me. It was obvious – I was being "watched" again. Unbelievable!

Representatives from the Church had made their views about me known, very clearly, in the national and local media. Then there had been the media statement by the Archbishop of Tuam, Dr Michael Neary, which warned people that, should they believe in these new apparitions, they could obscure the Shrine's message and "mislead" people.

It was evident that the representatives at Knock were, as usual, simply following orders. I don't hold any grudge. I keep them in my prayers at all times. I just wish they could keep an open mind and wait before they judge. Because the public do take what they say seriously and obey instructions to ignore these events. I believe people are being prevented from hearing the message that Our Lady is trying to communicate.

That's what bothers me more than anything. They are, through these kinds of media statement, denying people the right to access a real, genuine phenomenon – right now, when it is happening – denying people access to witness a series of apparitions which will continue and which, eventually, will be recognised in time by all churches around the world.

So, on this particular day, I had to ask myself: what did they think I was actually going to do that justified a security presence? Blow up the church?! Create a "bad influence" among churchgoers? Encourage people to look up at the sun? (This was the latest "stick" they had used to beat me with – that it was my fault if people looked up to see if the sun was spinning and dancing in the sky again! Something I had never instructed people to do.) Ignoring them all, and holding my head up high, I proceeded slowly and calmly into the church, which was almost full. There were about eighty people in all. I was deeply touched. I realised that those who had shown up were there because of their genuine belief in and love of God. They wanted to be present, yet again, to witness another apparition. They were singing the *Ave Maria* and in deep prayer as I entered the church.

At the altar, I placed the photo of Keith on the steps in front of the statue of Our Lady. Some of those attending then walked up to the altar, placed bunches of flowers at the foot of Keith's picture and said prayers. This was a very emotional time for me. Many of these lovely people had only met Keith once or twice, while most of them would have known him to see.

The Rosary then began and was recited out loud by about sixty people. Everyone joined in. There was a wonderful, loving atmosphere in the chapel, a sense of comradeship at a time of deep sorrow in the world, at a time in Ireland when we have virtually lost our faith, a nation that had once epitomised the very essence of what Catholicism was all about.

Most of those present were aware, of course, that as soon as the recital of the Holy Rosary would finish, at the end of the last decade, I would instantly drop to my knees and go into channel to receive the message from Our Lady. They prayed and waited with anticipation. A beautiful warm light seemed to glow in every corner of the church.

Just before the last two decades were recited, a young woman from Dublin, Danielle, who was sitting in the front row, heard a shuffling outside. She nudged her sister and a woman next to her and, looking out, they saw a priest and two lay people (one of whom was the main representative at Knock) entering a side door into the sacristy of the Apparition Chapel where we were praying. Suddenly a door into the chapel opened and a clerk shuffled out onto the altar, unannounced, and placed the missal in the centre of the altar. He then lit candles.

The Rosary continued.

The last decade of the rosary was about to be recited when there was a sudden unannounced interruption as a priest walked quickly out onto the altar. He immediately began to speak in a loud voice over a microphone. Speaking over the voices of those praying the Rosary, he proceeded to say Mass. No attempt was made on his part to wait until the Rosary had finished. No attempt was made to interrupt politely and explain that Mass was going to be said.

No one was aware that a Mass was to be said. There had been no announcement in advance. Open-mouthed, staring in utter disbelief at the events unfolding before them, those saying the Rosary quickly found their voices being drowned out by the priest's voice. Never looking up for one moment to his congregation, despite the fact that people were praying out loud, he continued, head bent.

Puzzled because of the speed of events and still not comprehending or taking in the situation, people started to question what was happening.

"Wasn't Mass supposed to be said in the other church at three o'clock?"

"Was a Mass scheduled to take place in the Apparition Church at 3.20 p.m.?"

"Are two Masses said during the week, off season, in both chapels, twenty minutes apart?"

Despite the fact that this was a renowned holy shrine, the pilgrimage season was over so very few people were about apart from myself and my followers. Why would there be two Masses, with a twenty-minute break between them, when there were so few people about to attend? None of this rang true at all!

Less than five minutes into the Mass, the priest began his sermon. As if to rub salt into the already festering wound, he then admonished those who might be "misled" into believing in supernatural occurrences, such as the spate of apparitions predicted in recent months. His sermon, nevertheless, fell on disbelieving and, in some quarters, deaf ears. People could not believe what they were hearing. The hypocrisy! The anger felt by all that day was palpable. Shocked and hurt, all of us were deeply upset at the way the apparition was "sabotaged", as one woman described it so aptly.

He read from a draft document in front of him, word for word. These were not his words, I'm sure of it now. He had been briefed. He had been instructed to speak before this particular group.

According to Denise Long from Galway, "Very soon after the Mass commenced I noticed that the priest couldn't get the words out, for some reason."

Soon after the Mass began so suddenly, a number of people noticed that the priest began to stutter, as if he couldn't remember the next words.

"He fumbled when opening the missal in front of him," said Therese Kelly. "He could see people crying with bitter disappointment that the Rosary was interrupted so unceremoniously. I think he must have felt embarrassed. I would like to think it was compassion, but I don't think so. It was so obvious to everyone there that this impromptu Mass was staged. A deliberate attempt to break up those attending and waiting for the apparition and for Joe Coleman to go into channel is how I saw it. How very sad, especially at a time when the Catholic Church could do with people of faith! I also noticed that the Mass was said very quickly – it was finished less than twenty minutes after it began. This had to be the fastest Mass I ever attended."

But as this drama unfolded, an extraordinary thing was happening in the church. Doreen Burke from

Dublin, along with three other people attending, recounted her incredible experience afterwards.

"I had been going to the apparitions since October 11th 2009. Each time I witnessed the dancing of the sun and I know what I saw was a cosmic miracle of the sun dancing the way it did. I became very close to Our Lady after that. I pray the Holy Rosary every day and attend church regularly.

"An extraordinary thing happened to me that day in the church, before the priest came in. As I prayed the Rosary 'from the heart' as Joe Coleman once told everyone, I could see the statue of Our Lady become misty. I began to stare. Was I imagining it? Then I saw her face begin to smile. *Couldn't be,* I thought. Suddenly the tears welled up in my eyes. They were tears of joy, not sadness. And I couldn't understand it. My body was absolutely still; I couldn't move. I felt very, very warm for some reason. I was looking up at the statue when I noticed that the face and body of Our Lady in the statue seemed to move to the right.

"Suddenly, I could see dazzling rays of light materialising around her body – right around her, on the outside of her body. Then she took on a human form. She became real. The statue remained, but she was a real person and was floating beside it. I couldn't stop whimpering. Crying. Overjoyed. Shocked. Then she seemed to be moving gently from side to side. You could say she floated. Speechless, I watched. She smiled but it wasn't a happy smile. It was a sad one.

All the lights around her were dazzling. I could see her beautiful dress, white and flowing, with what looked like a greyish blue gown over that. I couldn't see her feet.

"During this time, in the background, I could hear a man's voice begin to speak out loud. I knew it was a priest but I could not tear my eyes away from her. I continued to concentrate. But it was hard with the interruption. I felt a sense of love. I felt weak with emotion, as if I was seeing my own mother, who had died when I was a very young child.

"Then the link was broken. The sheer frustration that this wonderful contact with Our Lady was being interrupted in such a terrible way was so disappointing. Then she drifted away and all I could see was the statue. I looked up and noticed the priest trying to say the Mass. So upset and shocked was I that I ran out of the church, crying and shaking with shock. There were a few people about so I moved to the side of the church to get some privacy, so people wouldn't see me crying.

"Just then I looked up at the sky. And there it was again – the way it was at the last apparition. The sun was spinning. It had a dullish round centre that flashed in and out. It seemed to spin again and then flash getting smaller and then larger, moving all the time. There were no clouds in sight. It was a miracle. I was sad that I was one of so few to witness this extraordinary event."

Meanwhile, I remained in the Church for the entire Mass and at 3.40 p.m., when the Mass finished, I fell on my knees and looked up to see Our Lady. That day I was looking up at the stained-glass window above the altar when I saw her. She came to me in a soft cloud, her garments blowing. She was wearing a white robe with a blue cloak over it. When she came she was smiling but by the end of her message she was sad (details of this message are included in the following chapters). That day Our Lady was surrounded by angels of every kind imaginable. They were everywhere in the church. I could also see Archangel Michael and other saints, including Padre Pio.

I was in great form after that. I came out of the church surrounded by well-wishers and those seeking a healing, a cure. Many people reported that they had felt a marvellous presence in the church. Four people came forward and claimed they saw Our Lady; their stories are contained in the "Witnesses" chapter of this book.

Then someone shouted to me, "Joe, look up at the sun – it's at it again. You missed it when it started a while ago." I looked up and saw it dazzling, spinning, shaking and shimmering from side to side, as it does at most of the predicted apparitions, the ones where Our Lady tells me she will "make herself known". The crowd was enthralled. Some were praying openly, some crying, others had just such a happy smile on their faces. It was wonderful to watch, and watch it we did for a full forty-five minutes. The colours that came from it included a mix of orange, purple, blue and yellow – not the way the sun normally shines.

We saw one woman walk by the church, on the street outside, with a child in a buggy; she looked at us in wonder. *What are they looking at?* she must have said to herself. Then she turned around and looked up. We could hear her exclamation, though we were more than twenty feet away from her.

One man then shouted at the others, "Don't look up at the sun – that fella over there said it damages your eyes!" To our left we saw the Knock representatives, still at the security van and security guard gazing at us. I looked back over at him. The security man turned away. However, he came up to me much later, shook my hand, offered me his condolences over the death of Keith Henderson.

Afterward, walking around the town, we asked locals why there would be two Masses, twenty minutes apart on one day, in the middle of the week, off-season? Their answer? It doesn't happen! They couldn't understand it either.

We continued to discuss it in the local café.

Therese Kelly, still upset, said, "I could not believe that people from the Holy Shrine, set up in the first place in honour of the Blessed Virgin Mary, would behave like this. They deliberately used the Sacrament of Christ, the Holy Mass, to stop the Holy Rosary. It's a sacrilege in my view. We're all shocked and upset.

How dare they, when so few people have any faith left in the Church, go and behave like heathens? They didn't have the courtesy to apologise for the way they interrupted a private prayer group. I believe now, while the Catholic Church has good people working within its organisation, that they need to examine their consciences.

"Look, I am a Catholic. I still am. But as for the leadership? No. Most of them pussyfoot around what is right and wrong. They no longer have any leadership that would inspire you. They have no values any more. I think it will be up to us lay people to lead the way in the future. The leaders of the Catholic Church are too much into pomp and ceremony, elaborate costumes, hats, kissing hands, and jewels on their fingers! They have forgotten the true faith of the simple believers like us. They look at us as old-fashioned religious fanatics when we say the Rosary. They have no faith any more down here in Knock. Sure you only have to see the way they have cut the Rosary down to just one decade to see proof of that."

That day in Knock it came home to me, smack bang between the eyes. No matter how they dress it up, I believe that the Catholic hierarchy has lost their faith. They no longer have the strength to lead people into a strong powerful faith any more.

The contradiction of it all left me speechless and frustrated. I could barely find the words to express my outrage. Here we were at a time of great crisis in the Catholic Church and people, genuine holy people, were being treated in such a condescending manner. It came as no surprise, therefore, that these so-called representatives of the Church felt that they were divinely entrusted with the right to interrupt the recital of the Holy Rosary. The little respect they showed that day, not only for the devout prayer group but in the Holy Mass itself, was clearly evident. They showed no love of the congregation that day. No kindness to those with a deep faith. No; all they showed that day was lack of respect. Pure indifference disguised behind a cloak of religious piety. Their patronising, condescending attitude left all of us there with a sour taste in our mouths.

We followed up on the incident afterwards and were told that a "special Mass" had been requested for private intentions. As regards those who attended the Rosary in the Apparition Chapel, none of us had requested a special Mass. So what was this all about?

To use the holy Sacrament of the Mass to interrupt a devout prayer group's recital of the Holy Rosary is blasphemous in my opinion. But who do you complain to? We tried afterwards. Our complaints were played down. Ridiculed. "So are you saying that the Rosary is more important than the Mass?" we were asked. "Are you saying that these people 'objected' to a Mass being said?" This patronising response made me feel ill. Then we were told "This was a special Mass requested by people in the Apparition Chapel". When we found out later that this was untrue, they changed tactics. "What right did your group have to say the

Rosary in there?" we were asked. "You were not official nor invited pilgrims. We should not have to apologise for saying the Mass. It's our church, our shrine."

Afterwards, we had to ask: Who are the invited pilgrims? The elite among us that alone have the right to visit Knock? Do people need permission to enter the church? What kind of Church has this become? Who runs it? What is going on here?

You only have to look at the scandals in the Catholic Church today to gain a glimpse of the incredible distance they have put between themselves and the general public. How can you be expected to respect them? How can you expect them to believe in an apparition? How far removed from an acceptance of a supernatural occurrence, upon which many teachings are based, are they now? If that basis of belief is now gone, no longer relevant, that means they are lost. So many good priests have been sucked into this contradictory vacuum and are being forced to "toe the line".

What to believe in, then? If that fundamental belief is weakened, what then does the Church actually believe in? The biggest sadness, of course, is that their behaviour has destroyed people's belief in the Catholic Church.

But you should never turn away from God because of the Church. Their behaviour does not change the love God has for us. It does demonstrate the challenge between Satan and God. When Satan hurts the Church, he hurts God. If we believe that the Church is bad, because of the works of Satan, then we have been hoodwinked, and Satan has won. That's the part that makes me really sad.

Visions of the Future

14

World Disasters

During recent months, Our Lady has revealed to me a number of world disasters. I realise that I have got to be sensitive here, but she showed me, in advance, a vision of the first earthquake which took place in Turkey in the early hours of March 8th, 2010, and a follow-up second one which will happen at any time soon. I have also seen visions of some beautiful Western cities, razed to the ground, sophisticated modern cities, which I found hard to believe. Most of these cities I have never visited in my life. But she made it clear to me where they were and the names of these cities.

Shocked and deeply disturbed when she showed me these visions, I asked her, "Why, Mother, do you want to show me these things?" She explained that it was to show me what will happen as a result of people falling away from God in order to align themselves with the Antichrist and his values. She also informed me that these images represented what was in her Father's

Book. I presumed, naturally, she was referring to the prophecies relating to the Second Coming of Jesus Christ in the world.

I asked her, "How can we stop these events happening? Or can't we?"

She answered that prayer can help some of them from happening as can conversion. But, no, we can't stop all of them.

January 2010: Messages & Visions

The Vatican

On January 10th, Our Lady said:

> *"Satan will be no more. The evil one will be destroyed. He will live no more.*
>
> *"The hearts of my people will be filled with love for peace with the return of my Son, Jesus the Christ. For He will come back to the Earth through the Holy City of Jerusalem, which will shine like never before through many new suns and planets. It will shine so brightly. It will fill the hearts of many.*
>
> *"It is written in God's Book and prophesised many times through the centuries that the truth is hidden in the books beneath the vaults behind*

the Holy City and it will be received by all those who will come to praise God the Father – the true creator of all that is, seen and unseen. The angelic realm which comes back on the Earth, as it is now, is helping humanity."

Referring to Mount Calvary, where Jesus was crucified, she told me that the truth of Calvary will be revealed. I don't know what she meant by that.

Then I saw, in a vision, Pope Benedict being attacked physically in the Vatican. The message given to me was that he is in great danger and will be toppled. This could mean a physical assault or that he will lose control over the Vatican. She has kept reminding me, time and time again, that "Satan walks in the Vatican". This makes her very sad, because it is God's Church – the Church that he created. Satan, she explained, has brought this about to ensure that people stop believing in the Catholic Church.

Rio de Janeiro

She showed me Rio de Janeiro, where I could see a great manifestation of Jesus Christ. It will be a huge world event but it will be a good one. The people there, she tells me, are good people, devout and committed to the love of God, despite the problems they have had over the years.

End of the World

She also showed me a vision of the end of the Earth. I don't know if it was the whole Earth or just part of it. It was submerged in water – dark, black water. It was like looking at a vast never-ending ocean with no horizon. She also showed me fires burning, like a forest, a smouldering wilderness. This will happen, she told me, because of a large meteor which will fall out of the sky on this vast area of forest land. I can also clearly see in the vision lots of logs floating down the river.

I was told that if the world does not listen to the word of God, this is what is going to happen. She referred to it as the "Hand of Wrath" which will fall down like an axe to eradicate sin in the world. The Hand of God will come down harshly. God will do this because, if he doesn't, then Satan will take over the world. The battle has already begun. God will now fight the Deceiver head on.

It gave me so much comfort to hear that. There is hope after all. But without conversion, we won't be able to avoid some of the world disasters predicted I am afraid.

Vision of the Antichrist

I saw, in a very clear vision, the Antichrist, who will become a world leader – a very powerful, young, handsome and charismatic leader. He is here on the

Earth already. I am not sure what age he is right now, but in the vision I see him as a man in his late thirties. He will become a much-admired head of his country, with huge world influence. Charming and popular, he will emit a powerful positive glow but the messages he gives out will be false. People everywhere, Our Lady tells me, will praise him, be enthralled by him. And then the Deceiver will try to convert everyone to his way of thinking. He will be so convincing that people will have no reason to doubt him.

Because he will perform extraordinary things on the Earth, similar to what we would term as a "miracle sign", people will mistakenly believe that he has been sent from God. But he has not. Our Lady calls him the False Prophet. He will brainwash people to his way of thinking. She has also told me that the Muslim and Jewish people are already aware through their teachings of this man and are in no doubt that he will be revealed soon.

Our Lady warned me that the number 666 will be imprinted on the back of people's necks under the instructions of this leader. People will be stamped with this number and they will follow, because if they don't, he will have them killed. This could be a way of saying that a world leader will create a global political entity which will have control over people everywhere. Could it be a global alliance of some sort? I really don't understand the full implication of this. Nor do I know when this will happen.

The Antichrist will wear a red turban or headdress of some sort. Or perhaps "red" is meant as a symbol of some sort. In the vision she showed me of this man, I saw thousands of people, all wearing turbans, riding on horseback in the desert. A war had broken out and I could see lots of fighting. A huge army followed this leader.

The final image she showed me of him is that he is extremely wealthy, surrounded by oil and lives like a king in a palace in the desert.

But this was the interesting thing: as he deceives the world, all God's churches will come back and unite – this time as one in preparing to face the army of the Deceiver.

Message received on March 18th 2010

I dictated this while in channel as I was shown these visions:

- ***Ireland:*** Our Lady told me that the next day, March 19th 2010, would be a great day in Ireland. Because it is the Feast of St Joseph, people would be praying harder that day. That on this day a huge conversion would take place amongst people in Ireland. She also said that a great response, in time, would come from the Catholic Church to herald the new beginning of a new positive energy in the Church. She warned, however, that the Church would be rocked yet again, especially in Ireland. *(During this time there were strong calls on the primate of all Ireland Archbishop Seán Brady to resign.)*

- ***New York:*** She showed me a vision of St Patrick's Cathedral in New York. It looked, in my vision, as if it was crumbling. This could mean either the building will collapse or that another religious scandal will erupt. She has told me that they are not speaking the truth in the US and a lot of issues need to be sorted there.

- ***Germany:*** She told me that German Catholics will now start to go back to the Church again.

- ***Africa:*** 500 people are now working on behalf of Jesus Christ in Africa to bring conversion about in the lead-up to the Second Coming, and they are a powerful group.

- ***Hurricane:*** I saw some awful, disturbing images of a hurricane starting on a small island, somewhere where there are palm trees. It won't be a huge hurricane. I could see the winds moving at high speed and I could see children dying. I saw small shacks like caravans being blown apart. I have no idea when this will happen.

- ***Bangkok:*** I could see another disaster in Thailand; I think it's in Bangkok. The devil, she tells me, is rampant there and children are the victims. I don't know when this is going to happen, but it will.

- ***Suicides:*** Sadly, she showed me suicides – the suicides of priests in Ireland and elsewhere. Many innocent priests are so ashamed of what is going on in the Church that they will not be able to stand the pressure. She is very sad about this, she told me.

- ***New Planet:*** This was probably the most amazing vision yet. She showed me a new planet, like a bigger more spectacular version of the sun. It will be seen by the naked eye. She told me that there are people who know these things already, but are keeping it secret and will not go public with it. But it will happen.

- ***Our Lady*** told me that people all over Ireland will see, clearly, a number of black crosses in the sky. It will be seen not just in Knock but all over Ireland. A similar phenomenon will be seen in other countries. Conversion is taking place in Ireland but it needs to be much quicker. Ireland will be the focus of world attention, as it will be seen as showing an example to the rest of the world in its devotion to prayer in order to save souls on this Earth. Other countries will follow suit.

- ***The Vatican:*** She referred again to books in the Holy City. There are books "in my Father's House" in Rome, she said. She told me that the Holy See will bring out and reveal the secrets they contain. That cleansing, where the truth will be revealed, has already started. These books will be brought out into the open and the revelations, written thousands of years ago, which the world is not aware of, will finally be shown.

- ***The Rapture:*** Our Lady has reminded me that the believers and their families will be lifted when the cleansing takes place and Heaven comes to Earth as St Paul said to the Thessalonians: "*We who are alive on the day the Lord comes will not go ahead of those who have died. There will be the shout of command, the archangel's voice, the sound of God's trumpet, and the Lord himself will come down from heaven. Those who have died believing will be gathered up along with them in the clouds to meet the Lord in the air. And so we will always be with the Lord.*" (1 Thessalonians 4)

Message received on March 22nd, 2010
12.45 p.m. home

"Hello, my dear child. Peace be with you. Today I will speak of the Second Coming of my beloved

Son, the Son of God, Jesus the Christ, King of the Earth, King of All Nations, King of Israel. My Son's Coming will be like the first. He will come in glory. He comes before the Last Judgement. The hour and the time are not for your knowing for they are written in the secrets of the Almighty Father. My dear child of God, the world will be consumed in total darkness due to the rejection and denial and disbelief of God, the Most Holy and Powerful One. Jesus the Son of God, when he comes, will find faith on Earth. So suddenly will he come that my people, my children, will not be ready. This is why it is very important that my holy priests listen and heed my most urgent messages. You, my child, must go and inform them. They will and must listen to you, my child.

"Do not be taken aback by my words. Trust in everything, my child. I am your beloved Mother. I walk before you in everything you do, my sweet child. I am the Immaculate Conception. I am your Mother. You must know this. You must feel me in your heart. Take shelter, my sweet child, today and every day, under the mantle of your Immaculate Mother. Peace be with you. Go now and pray my most Holy Rosary.

"Peace be with you. Mother of Peace. Mary, Mother of Love."

2.25 p.m.

"My dear child, you say my most Holy Rosary with so much love and devotion from your heart. You have so much faith now, my sweet child. Peace be yours, my beloved child.

"Father Seamus will help you with your work. He already knows this for he knows you have been praying for him. Continue to pray for him and for all my Son's disciples worldwide. Please pray for Pope Benedict and all in the Holy See. Pray that Satan will not get his grip on my Son's consecrated disciples. My child, your prayers are powerful and most strong. You must teach my people, my children, how to have and hold their faith. Show them how to pray from their hearts. My child, it is of great importance against our battle against the Serpent. For it helps when multitudes pray together from their hearts. It has great strength and power to squash the Deceiver. I have told you many times, my child, you have been chosen to go forth with my message. Many have been chosen but only the strong have been picked. For you, my sweet child, have been given the graces to do my work. You do not question me. For you believe in your spirit and you know in your heart I am your Immaculate Mother. Go now, my child. I bless you in the Name of the

Father and of the Son and of the Holy Spirit. Amen. Go forth in peace and love.

"Mary, Mother of Jesus the Christ. Mother of Peace. Mother, Queen of Heaven. Mother, Queen of Ireland."

Making Sense of Knock's Opposition

15

Making Sense of Knock's Opposition

Comparisons with Original Apparition

The Archbishop of Tuam, Michael Neary, has published his views on the apparitions I have predicted and which took place in Knock during 2009 and 2010. He emphatically rejected the reports of the apparitions, yet he wasn't even there in person. On October 26th 2009, five days before the apparition on October 31st, he issued the following statement online and through the national print media:

> *Knock is a much-loved place of pilgrimage and prayer. Ever since the apparition in 1879, believers from home and abroad have made the pilgrimage there in increasing numbers. The most renowned of all pilgrims to the Shrine of Our Lady of Knock was his Holiness, Pope John Paul II, who came for the centenary of the shrine*

in 1979, thus reaching "the goal of his journey to Ireland" where he was able to "make yet another pilgrimage to the Shrine of the Mother of Christ, the Mother of the Church, the Queen of Peace" (Homily at Mass in Knock, 30 September 1979).

The great gift of Knock consists in a particular way in prayer and the celebration of the sacraments, in penance and the conversion of life. "All those who have come to Knock have received blessings through the intercession of Mary . . . The sick and suffering, people handicapped in body and in mind, troubled in their faith or their conscience, all have been healed, comforted and confirmed in their faith because they trusted that the Mother of God would lead them to her Son Jesus" (Pope John Paul II). It is this trust in the Mother of God, this turning to her divine Son, borne out in the practical care of the sick, and in the celebration of the sacraments of reconciliation, anointing and Eucharist, that lie at the core of the Knock pilgrimage.

For one hundred and thirty years now, the pilgrims to Knock have been pilgrims in faith. They "walk by faith and not by sight" to quote the words of St Paul (II Corinthians 5:7). *This is their great blessing, the blessing in fact that Jesus mentions to the doubting Thomas: they have not seen and still they believe* (John 20:29).

The Authentic Identity of the Shrine

Such faith makes Knock pilgrims firm in hope and active in love for the sick and suffering. They do not expect visions or seek further apparitions. God has manifested Himself in Jesus Christ and His people have responded ever since. Unfortunately, recent events at the Shrine obscure this essential message. They risk misleading God's people and undermining faith. For this reason, such events are to be regretted rather than encouraged.

My response to this? No one, especially the Catholic Church, ever believes in visionaries – first time round. They didn't believe in the visionaries at Knock at the first apparition and waited fifty-seven years before it was accepted as authentic!

They question and question. I suppose on the one hand they are right to do this. Because, after all, anyone can make such a claim. If it was just based on my claims, then I could understand. But why did the Church not listen to so many hundreds of people who claimed to have seen the sun, on four separate occasions at the exact time and date of the predicted apparitions, "dance" in the sky in a very unusual way? Why did they have to dismiss their views? Witness reports were all similar. You could very easily look at the sun on those days at 3.20 p.m. exactly. It was not glaring, because a mesh-like disc seemed to hover over it. Could they not have kept an open mind?

Why does the Church today, despite their own embarrassing scandals, feel they can dismiss such claims so vehemently? Not one bishop or priest attended the apparitions I predicted, yet they declared the events inauthentic. They simply waved off any such claims with a swift dismissal as being not worthy of discussion.

Some day they will understand. Some day they will acknowledge what happened. Some day they will accept these apparitions as being authentic. All of this sounds so familiar. Reaction to Medjugorje was the same. It happened in Fatima and, indeed, when the first apparition in Knock itself was reported!

Comparison with Original Apparition

The Archbishop of Tuam today would do well to go back in time and consider what happened in Knock all those years ago. His predecessor, the Most Rev Dr John MacHale, the Archbishop of Tuam, in 1879 set up a Commission of Inquiry within six weeks of the original apparition. But it wasn't until 1936, fifty-seven years later that the apparitions were considered "trustworthy and satisfactory"! So if the Archbishop of Tuam's intention is to prove that the first apparition was always considered authentic from day one, then everyone has been seriously misled.

Fifteen witnesses in 1879 were examined to seek an explanation that could sit well with the Catholic

Church. The witnesses were not believed and were continuously questioned. It wasn't until 1936 that a second Commission was held, while three of the witnesses were still living, which confirmed the original findings. One of the witnesses, Mrs Mary O'Connell (Mary Byrne) gave evidence under oath from her deathbed. She claimed, "I am quite clear about everything I have said, and I make this statement knowing I am going before my God."

Despite the Church's reluctance to accept the claims made by the fifteen witnesses to the original apparition, the first organised pilgrimage to Knock came from Limerick in 1880 and was welcomed by the Most Rev Dr John MacHale at the time (despite the ongoing investigation). He is recorded as saying at that time: "It is a great blessing to the poor people of the West, in their wretchedness, misery and sufferings, that the Blessed Virgin Mother of God has appeared among them." From the time the apparition was first reported, pilgrims have been coming to the shrine despite the fact that the Church did not acknowledge the authenticity of the original claims of the witnesses. Hundreds of cures were reported at the time among the sick and disabled, who made this journey of hope during the last years of the nineteenth century.

So what's different this time? Nothing really. The Church still deny anything is happening. They still oppose. But this time they didn't attend the predicted apparitions on the day they were to happen. They refused to even consider what I had to say. Odd, that; surely even curiosity would have got the better of them? No; they just weren't interested. They would rather condemn my claims as nonsense instead.

Today, the original Knock phenomenon and its final acceptance is based on the same type of apparition. The irony escapes those who work in Knock today. I feel sorry for the Catholic Church today. I pray for it. I pray for the many genuine good priests, bishops, cardinals and nuns. Why? Because I believe that Satan has infiltrated the Catholic Church. The saddest thing of all is that this is what he wanted to achieve. To undermine the Church. And he has won – to a certain extent. There is still the faith of the people to contend with. People with strong faith won't be beaten. And now you have the Catholic Faith itself being undermined because of the corruption displayed by the very apostles who represent it.

I only hope that ordinary people will understand that it is the corrupt few in the Catholic Church who are responsible. God is not to blame.

Despite my sending them the messages I have received from Our Lady they simply ignored them. They were not worth the paper they were written on is the clear message I have received. I was simply dismissed as being a crank. I was belittled. Blamed for bringing shame on a Holy Shrine. I was even blamed for the lack of security on October 31st 2010 (where they had been warned in advance of the huge likely attendance) and, indeed, the litter they found after the event. No mention of the messages.

Writing this even now, I can still feel the pain, humiliation and hurt of that day, the 31st October 2010 at Knock. Not so much for the way I was treated, which was to be expected, but for the way the thousands of believers were treated and treated publicly because they believed that an apparition was going to take place.

The views of the Catholic Church and other sceptics were made clear in the numerous media reports at the time, many of which can still be viewed online today.

This is my assessment of the views expressed and the statements issued at the time:

- It is okay to pay homage to an apparition which took place in the past. But God forbid we might honour an apparition that takes place in modern Ireland. No, that wouldn't do.

- No apparition will take place next week.

- Such events are to be regretted rather than encouraged.

- There is nothing scheduled in the Basilica for tomorrow. It is open but there is nothing else going on. (This was announced the day before when we estimated that up to 10,000 people would show up)

- Pilgrims at Knock do not expect visions or seek further apparitions.
- A priest will not be available to recite the Rosary with Joe Coleman or the thousands gathered.
- The statue of Our Lady will not be allowed into the Basilica Church – only when official pilgrims are there. And certainly not outside of the 'Pilgrim' season.
- Microphones are not allowed in the Church for pilgrims who show up expecting to see an apparition.
- People who look at the sun long enough "imagine things".
- No apparition occurred. We didn't see anything.
- How dare people leave litter in the Church?
- The Church may have to take an injunction against the people who made the prediction.
- A very dangerous situation occurred with thousands fleeing from the church to see the sun "dance" in the sky outside.
- The type of people who showed up were not the "usual" pilgrims. The church is reserved only for those who are part of an "official" pilgrimage

Every possible effort was made to urge people *not* to attend on the day through various media statements. The prediction I made was declared to be downright false beforehand. Apparitions just don't happen in modern Ireland. Yes – the Church does accept that the original apparition took place in Knock. But not one that might – just might – be taking place before their very eyes.

My heart went out to the thousands who gathered there that day. Many were so hurt, frustrated and insulted that they were not given the courtesy of being allowed to hear the Most Holy Rosary said in the Basilica Church that day. Here they were, in their thousands, trying to pray out loud but no one could hear because the microphones had been turned off in advance. This seemed mean-spirited even to the skeptics.

The view expressed afterwards was that the entire event, where people reported that the sun began to spin in the sky, was simply an "optical illusion". But, of course, it was not surprising. After all, they said the same about the seventy thousand people who witnessed a similar event in Fatima.

So the official view was declared. No, there was no apparition at Knock on the October 31st 2009. Claims made by Catholic Church representatives, who were not present on the day, littered the media for weeks afterwards. Witnesses among the ten thousand people there who claimed they saw the sun spinning and dancing in the sky were "imagining" it. That's all. Nothing to worry about.

This is exactly the position that has been taken time and time again by the Catholic Church since apparitions of Our Lady were first reported from around the world. They reacted in exactly the same way at Lourdes (France), in Fatima (Portugal); Garabandal (Spain); right through to the more recent apparitions in Medjugorje. All of the visionaries were ridiculed and disbelieved. Every single time. None of them were believed. Until afterwards.

Even if the Catholic Church feels the need to exert caution, and this is understandable to a point, I was stunned that they expressed such outright condemnation in the way they did. It would have been so much easier to let people make up their own minds. But, above all, they should have treated the faithful with respect instead of outright condemnation for daring to believe in any kind of supernatural occurrence which, after all, is what the Catholic Church proclaims to believe in.

At a time when fewer Catholics are attending Mass, and when so many have turned their backs on the Catholic Church, I would have thought that Catholics who believe in a Marian Apparition and who wanted to witness Our Lady would have been accommodated. Calmly and in a controlled secure manner. This was not the case sadly.

As for the travelling community who are renowned for their devotion to Our Lady – what happened to them when they showed up in Knock on the previous Friday leaves many questions that still need to be answered. Nothing was done to facilitate their stay – indeed, everything was done to discourage them.

While it will take some time for the Catholic Church to understand what is happening in Knock, let's just imagine for one minute what will actually happen when Jesus returns to the Earth. Will his prophets be believed? I doubt it. Will he, himself, be believed? No, I don't think so. The last time he came to Earth he was tormented and mocked unmercifully before he was finally murdered. Christians must now be honest with themselves. Would they accept Jesus today? Would they accept a message he sent through his Blessed Mother in advance? Would they listen?

So what will be different the next time around? Will the very Church that proclaims a belief in the miracles that happened during Jesus's lifetime, His resurrection from the dead, and His promise that He will come back again to judge the living and dead, believe this when it finally happens? The second time around?

And so, today, as I write this, I learn that the Vatican is finally investigating events at Medjugorje, some thirty years after the first apparitions were reported. How come? Why so late?

The Most Urgent Message of all

16

March 10th 2010, 3.40 p.m.

The day of March 10th 2010 at Knock was significant in more ways than one. Our Lady gave me a message that day which would be the subject of much publicity afterwards. Because this was the most powerful message I had received to date. And it presented me with one of the biggest challenges I have had to face so far.

"Blessings, my sweet child.

"Today I surround you and give you many graces. I take away the hurt you carry in your heart. You're stronger now, my loved one. Stronger than before. You are surrounded with God's love and protection. All of your angels are here with you today not because you desire them to be but because they decide to be with you today to ease your burden.

"It is my Father's will that you be strong for your work. For you, my sweet child, the heavens have opened. You will feel much stronger now; peace with you. You notice today I have tears in my eyes. I am sad for my priests here at Knock. You must tell my children to continue to pray for them with all your heart.

"Today my most Holy Rosary was interrupted. The work of the Deceiver. This was a test for my people. Tell them they must not let this distract from saying my most powerful Holy Rosary, as the power of prayer makes the Evil One cringe.

"My child, the time has come now for conversion. Changes have begun, especially here at Knock. I have told you many times that the foundations have been rocked. They will continue to be rocked worldwide.

"My son, Jesus the Christ, hurts so much when his beloved consecrated disciples disobey His Father´s commandments. My sweet child, my message must go out to my people worldwide, for this is most urgent.

"My people must gather in multitudes at the Holy Shrine in Knock on Tuesday 11th May 2010. My Holy Rosary must be recited at 2 p.m. in all churches throughout Ireland.

"I request that Holy Mass be said at 3 p.m. sharp.

"I request my children to receive reconciliation before Mass and everyone receive the Body, the Blood and Divinity of my beloved Son, Jesus the Christ. It is most urgent that my message be heeded. The Deceiver must not be allowed to take control of my Church. Pray. Pray. Pray every day, every day.

"Pray for non-believers.

"Pray for lost souls in purgatory.

"Especially pray for my bishops, priests, prayer groups, lay people, all over Ireland.

"My child, Ireland needs prayer now at this time of great change. It is of great urgency that my message be heeded. You, my dear child of God, have been given permission to spread my message. Do not worry, my child, for your work is very much in God's Hand.

"Thank you for responding today. Go now in peace and love. I am your Blessed Mother. Mother of Jesus the Christ. Mother of Love and Compassion. Mary Queen of Heaven.

[pause]

[final parting words]

"Jesus said souls that eat his flesh possess God.

"Love thy neighbour as I have loved you.

I was shocked by the urgency of this message. Immediately I knew I had to take action. I knew I would need all the graces and prayers to pluck up the courage to bring this message, not only to the Catholic Church, but to ordinary people, not only in Ireland but around the world. So the first step I took was to contact the Most Rev Diarmuid Martin, Archbishop of Dublin, Primate of Ireland.

This is the letter I dictated on March 14th 2010, which was eventually delivered by courier to his residence on March 19th 2010.

Most Rev Diarmuid Martin,
Archbishop of Dublin,
Primate of Ireland
Archbishop's Residence,
Drumcondra,
Dublin 9

Ref: Reported Apparitions at Knock Holy Shrine 2009–2010 (and ongoing)

May I respectfully request, as a genuine visionary and seer for Our Blessed Mother, that you read the enclosed message I received from Our Lady during an apparition which took place in Knock, on 10 March 2010 at 3.40 p.m. I ask that you do this with an open mind. The matter is urgent because I have been asked by Our Lady to present it to the Catholic Church without fail.

I am a 56-year-old working-class man from Ballyfermot, Dublin, a genuine visionary for Our Blessed Mother, Our Lady, for some time. While I have kept details of my visions private it is only since last October 2009 that Our Lady has instructed me to reveal details of a series of apparitions, in Knock, County Mayo, along with messages she gives me.

For the record I would like to clarify and confirm the following:

1. *I am not a fraud. The apparitions I am privy to are of divine origin. I have no doubt that false claims of visions of Jesus and the Virgin Mary and so-called messages are common. I can understand why the Vatican has to be sceptical about reported apparitions and why they would be concerned about the increase in same. I respect these views.*

2. *I am not a pseudo-mystic. Our Lady has, however, shown me visions of world catastrophes which feature, clearly, the current Pope, His Holiness*

Pope Benedict – all of which are very distressing. I dictated details and dates of these to a witness, all of which were documented last in November 2009. Sadly, one of the visions, which involved a world earthquake, has proven to be correct.

3. *My objective is not to embarrass or cause any damage to the Catholic Church. I am a Catholic myself and would hate to see any further damage caused to the Church as a result of these messages. But see them you must.*

4. *I just want the messages to be (a) read by senior representatives of the Catholic Church in Ireland and in Rome and (b) given a fair hearing before they are dismissed out of hand.*

5. *The Catholic Church feels happier, I have heard, when visionaries are being "checked out" that priests with special skills are used to interview them. In many instances the first thing they look for is demonic possession. In the past the Church has tended to use priests with strong exorcist powers to examine such people. So when I received a call from a representative of a renowned spiritual director and exorcist to see him in relation to the apparitions in Ireland, I immediately agreed. In November 2009 I went to London where he had been hosting a special retreat and met him privately.*

It was an experience I will never forget. This man, I believe, can look into a person's soul. Blessed with the Holy Spirit, it is said he has the ability to know instantly whether someone is genuine or not. I felt an immense love from this holy man and I was thankful and honoured when he subsequently declared me to be an authentic visionary and seer for Our Lady.

6. *A series of supernatural phenomena DID take place at the Holy Shrine in Knock which include scenes of the sun "dancing in the sky" for up to 45–50 minutes – covered over by a metallic white disc with a black but faint ring around it – where it dazzled, gyrated and began spinning. Hundreds of witnesses will acknowledge this. They took place on the following dates: 11 October 2009; 31 October 2009; 22 February 2010; and 10 March 2010. All were witnessed and verified by various people and were interviewed by The Media.*

7. *There are now a number of witnesses, all unknown to each other, who have come forward confirming how the miracle of the sun has converted them back to believing in God again. In addition, a number of cures have been reported.*

My job is not to convert the world. I am simply the messenger. My job is to make sure people hear the messages – the ones Our Lady wants to be revealed. The reason I am contacting you now is that the last message is urgent. Our Lady has urged me to hand it over to the Catholic Church without fail.

Nor am I an attention-seeker. It is because of my deep love for Our Blessed Mother that I have had to go public with the apparitions – much to my family's discomfort.

I do not seek publicity for myself. I can't stand it, to tell you the truth. I'm not well-versed in dealing with the media. In fact, I have lost my temper I don't know how many times during media interviews and this has made me look bad. But I have a duty and I would do anything Our Lady tells me to do.

I now enclose this last message, received on 10 March 2010. In addition, I enclose all the other messages to date for your immediate consideration and inspection. You are the FIRST member of the Catholic Church hierarchy to receive same.

I would also be grateful if you could advise as to how I can ensure that they are issued to the Vatican.

Finally, would you be kind enough to meet with

me, along with a close personal friend, respected in the business community, in your offices for a private consultation in the strictest of confidence?

I respectfully await your comments and would appreciate if your office could let me know immediately if this is in order.

In conclusion, may I also respectfully request that if you or your colleagues have no interest in following up on this, would you be kind enough to let me know.

Yours sincerely,
Joe Coleman

Background Information on Joe Coleman, Visionary & Seer for Our Lady

"In his own words"

- *Age 56 years from Ballyfermot, Co. Dublin.*
- *Left school at 13 years of age, consider myself extremely poor with very little money to live on.*
- *Unemployed and on disability benefit for 30 years (due to a serious back and spinal injury).*

- *Blessed with ability to communicate with spirits from a very young age, I have always had a very strong devotion to Our Lady and Jesus Christ. Saw my first apparition of Our Lady when I was 12 years of age. Have been having visions of her for many, many years but kept them private and only revealed details to my immediate friends and family for fear of being ridiculed.*

- *These visions have brought me very close to Our Lady and there was no reason to share these messages or visions up to now.*

- *I have been blessed with spiritual healing powers, which has seen a large number of people, many of whom had terminal illnesses, cured immediately. This, of course, I realise is not me – it is the hand of God. I am simply a channel.*

- *I am dyslexic. Never read a Bible in my life and, up to recently, did not know how to recite the full Holy Rosary. I am not proud of this; I know very few prayers – I make most of them up, although I am learning fast. Our Lady has given me personal prayers that I say now.*

- *I now believe I urgently need a spiritual director in my work with Mother but not sure where I can go to find this person.*

- *Where to from here? I really don't know. I never know when Our Lady appears to me when the next apparition is to take place until I receive the message, in channel, immediately after the apparition.*

- *I now attend Mass seven days a week, I receive the Body of Christ once a day, holy confession once a month, I attend twice a week the Adoration, I receive Benediction every Friday and I pray the Holy Rosary every day for lost souls and for non-believers, and in particular the priests and the bishops and the holy Catholic Church.*

- *RTÉ have just completed a documentary which will be aired in the summer. Archbishop Michael Neary, who issues public statements denouncing me and my work, refused to be interviewed for the programme.*

I sent off this letter and then I sat back and waited. And I waited.

And just as I expected – there has been no response.

17

A Seer, a Mystic, a Visionary . . . What am I?

The Bible tells us that a prophet is a person who has access to the supernatural or the divine. It also shows us that it can be someone who acts as an intermediary to communicate messages from the spiritual plane to the human race.

I believe I am such a person. And I mean this in the most humble way possible. I am deeply honoured and touched beyond belief that Our Lady has chosen me to give her messages to the world. Out of pure love and reverence for God the Almighty Father, I see my role as not just a matter of communicating the messages He is sending to us, through His Blessed Mother but also as encouraging all of us to pray for all souls to be saved.

With the special graces I have been privileged to receive, along with other visionaries throughout the world, my job is to promote change and action needed globally in order to fight the Evil One and his army of followers in preparation for the Second Coming.

I consider myself a vessel for God and the power I have been blessed with comes from God above. No one else. That brings its own responsibilities.

As part of my work I have been given visions of the future from Our Lady, and have been shown certain revelations relating to the Second Coming of Jesus the Christ (as she refers to him) on Earth, events which are not yet known by the masses. It is a hard, lonely path to follow and one which brings a barrage of abuse in its wake. But I accept it willingly and will continue to forge ahead with what I have been asked to do.

My main role, through the messages of Our Lady, is to remind the world of the truth. The truth of our faith, the truth that is God and the words contained in her "Father's Book" as she continually refers to the Bible. It is only the truth that will set the world free from the Evil One – towards the new Heaven on Earth promised to us by Jesus, who suffered on the cross to save us all.

My faith has had to grow as part of my test. The torment that has followed is, I realise now, part of that challenge. Just because I have the gift of channel, where I can see Our Lady and angels of the higher realm just as I can see other people in the flesh, it does not mean I was equipped to handle this. Not at all. I had to learn the hard lessons, from Our Lady, that come with this gift. It wasn't easy. It has been extremely difficult for me personally but, through the grace of God, I have learned to live with it. The joy it brings as well as the suffering cannot be separated. They are one.

Why Our Lady came to me in the first place is unknown to me. I am not a learned person. I have very little money with which to promote these messages. Without her help and that of the wonderful Light Workers whom she has sent to spread the message, I would have found it much more difficult.

Our Lady keeps me strong through her daily messages. So too does the Archangel Michael, who is always at my side to help me through the periods of doubt I may have or when I am faced with fear and the evils that this work brings with it.

I will continue with my work to spread word from Our Lady and, despite the opposition I will receive, to encourage people to attend the Holy Shrine in Knock for the apparitions.

Our Lady has taught me all the ways we can bring Jesus into our lives and, in particular, the importance of her Holy Rosary. As Padre Pio once said of the Rosary, "Mary put a sword into the hands of her children, and that sword is the Rosary."

One young woman said to me recently, "Joe, I really believe now in Our Lady and what's happening at Knock. But I don't know how to pray and don't know the words of the Rosary." For her, and for all the young people in Ireland, as well as the generations around the world who have forgotten how to pray, I have written the following "Guide to Saying the Rosary".

A Guide to Saying the Holy Rosary

18

About the Rosary

"Rosary" comes from a Latin word meaning a garland of roses or a "crown of roses". The rosary is the symbol that represents Our Lady and it is powerful because it's a prayer that groups of people can say together. It is all about asking Our Lady to pray for us and for others. It is extremely powerful because, whatever Our Lady asks of Jesus, he can never say no to her, once the intention is of a divine nature.

The Rosary lost its popularity after Vatican II but has finally made a comeback, not just amongst the Catholic population but within the Protestant community. They now see the relevance of the Rosary as an ideal form of prayer that helps to fight the Evil One. It will help bring about our salvation.

Our Lady revealed fifteen promises for those who pray the Rosary to the Dominican Blessed Alan de la Roche in the fifteenth century.

1. To all those who shall pray my Rosary devoutly, I promise my special protection and great graces.

2. Those who shall persevere in the recitation of my Rosary will receive some special grace.

3. The Rosary will be a very powerful armour against Hell; it will destroy vice, deliver from sin and dispel heresy.

4. The Rosary will make virtue and good works flourish, and will obtain for souls the most abundant divine mercies. It will draw the hearts of men from the love of the world and its vanities, and will lift them to the desire of eternal things. Oh, that souls would sanctify themselves by this means!

5. Those who trust themselves to me through the Rosary will not perish.

6. Whoever recites my Rosary, devoutly reflecting on the Mysteries, shall never be overwhelmed by misfortune. He will not experience the anger of God nor will he perish by an unprovided death. The sinner will be converted; the just will persevere in grace and merit eternal life.

7. Those truly devoted to my Rosary shall not die without the sacraments of the Church.

8. Those who are faithful to recite my Rosary

shall have during their life and at their death the light of God and the plenitude of His graces and will share in the merits of the blessed.

9. I will deliver promptly from purgatory souls devoted to my Rosary.

10. True children of my Rosary will enjoy great glory in heaven.

11. What you shall ask through my Rosary you shall obtain.

12. To those who propagate my Rosary I promise aid in all their necessities.

13. I have obtained from my Son that all the members of the Rosary Confraternity shall have as their intercessors, in life and in death, the entire celestial court.

14. Those who recite my Rosary faithfully are my beloved children, the brothers and sisters of Jesus Christ.

15. Devotion to my Rosary is a special sign of predestination.

How to Say the Rosary

The Rosary comprises a set of different prayers as follows and must, ideally, be said holding a set of Rosary beads. Meditation during the Rosary is vital. It is important to meditate on each mystery associated with each decade of the Rosary. It's not enough to recite the prayers, because if you don't focus on each mystery of the Rosary while you are saying it, this only scratches the surface of what it is really all about. The Rosary is not just about the recitation of prayers, which for many people can seem boring, because it can become meaningless repetition. You need to concentrate on each of the mysteries and try to imagine yourself in the situation that the mystery reveals.

The Mysteries of the Rosary

The Joyful Mysteries (Mondays and Thursdays; Sundays of Advent):

1. *The Annunciation:* Mary learns from the Angel Gabriel that God wishes her to be the mother of Jesus and humbly accepts. (Luke 1:26–38)
2. *The Visitation:* Mary goes to visit her cousin Elizabeth and is praised by her as "blessed among women". (Luke 1:39–56)
3. *The Nativity:* Mary gives birth to Jesus in the stable at Bethlehem. (Luke 2:1–20)

4. *The Presentation:* Mary and Joseph present Jesus to His Heavenly Father in the Temple of Jerusalem forty days after His birth. (Luke 2:22–39)

5. *The Finding in the Temple:* After searching for three days, Mary and Joseph find the twelve-year-old Jesus sitting in the Temple discussing the law with the learned doctors. (Luke 2:42–52)

The Sorrowful Mysteries (Tuesdays and Fridays; Sundays of Lent)

1. *The Agony in the Garden:* The thought of our sins and His coming suffering causes the agonising Saviour to sweat blood (*haematidrosis*). (Luke 22:39–44)

2. *The Scourging:* Jesus is stripped and unmercifully scourged until His body is one mass of bloody wounds. (Matthew. 27:26)

3. *The Crowning with Thorns:* Jesus' claim to kingship is ridiculed by putting a crown of thorns on His head and a reed in His hand. (Matthew. 27:28–31)

4. *The Carrying of the Cross:* Jesus shoulders His own cross and carries it to the place of crucifixion while Mary follows Him, sorrowing. (Luke 23:26–32)

5. *The Crucifixion:* Jesus is nailed to the cross and dies after three hours of agony witnessed by His Mother. (Matthew. 27:33-50)

The Glorious Mysteries (Sundays except during Advent and Lent, Wednesdays and Saturdays)

1. *The Resurrection:* Jesus rises from the dead on Easter Sunday, glorious and immortal, as He has predicted. (Matthew. 28:1–7)

2. *The Ascension:* Jesus ascends into Heaven forty days after His resurrection to sit at the right hand of God the Father. (Luke 24:50–51)

3. *The Descent of the Holy Spirit:* Jesus sends the Holy Spirit in the form of fiery tongues on His Apostles and disciples. (Acts 2:2–4)

4. *The Assumption:* Mary, having completed the course of her earthly life, is assumed body and soul into heavenly glory.

5. *The Coronation:* Mary is crowned as Queen of Heaven and Earth, Queen of Angels and Saints.

The Luminous Mysteries (The Light Mysteries) (Thursdays)

1. *The Baptism in the Jordan:* John the Baptist baptizes Jesus. After Jesus' baptism a voice from Heaven says, "This is my beloved Son in whom I am well pleased." (Matthew 3:17)

2. *The Wedding at Cana*: At Mary's request, Jesus works His first miracle by changing the water into wine. (John 2:1–12)

3. *The Proclamation of the Kingdom:* "My kingdom is not of this world." (John 18:36)

4. *The Transfiguration:* Jesus takes Peter, James and John up a high mountain to pray and is transfigured before them. "His face became as dazzling as the sun, his clothes as radiant as light." (Luke 9:35)

5. *The Institution of the Eucharist:* "Whoever eats my flesh and drinks my blood remains in me and I in him." (John 13:1)

The Prayers

The Sign of the Cross

In the name of the Father, and of the Son, and of the Holy Spirit. Amen.

The Apostles' Creed

I believe in God, the Father Almighty, creator of Heaven and Earth; and in Jesus Christ, His only Son, our Lord; Who was conceived by the Holy Ghost, born of the Virgin Mary, suffered under Pontius Pilate, was crucified, died and was buried. He descended into Hell. On the third day He rose again; He ascended into Heaven, and sitteth at the right hand of God, the Father Almighty; from thence He shall come to judge the living and the dead. I believe in the Holy Ghost, the Holy Catholic Church, the communion of saints, the forgiveness of sins, the resurrection of the body, and life everlasting. Amen.

Our Father

Our Father, Who art in heaven, hallowed be Thy name; Thy kingdom come; Thy will be done on Earth as it is in Heaven. Give us this day our daily bread; and forgive us our trespasses as we forgive those who trespass against us; and lead us not into temptation, but deliver us from evil. Amen.

Hail Mary

Hail Mary, full of grace. The Lord is with thee. Blessed art thou amongst women, and blessed is the fruit of thy womb, Jesus. Holy Mary, Mother of God, pray for us sinners, now and at the hour of our death. Amen.

Glory Be

Glory be to the Father, and to the Son, and to the Holy Spirit. As it was in the beginning, is now, and ever shall be, world without end. Amen.

Fatima Prayer (Optional)

O my Jesus, forgive us our sins. Save us from the fires of Hell. Lead all souls to heaven, especially those in most need of thy mercy.

HAIL HOLY QUEEN

Hail, Holy Queen, Mother of Mercy; our life, our sweetness and our hope. To thee do we cry, poor banished children of Eve: to thee do we send up our sighs, mourning and weeping in this valley of tears. Turn then, most gracious advocate, thine eyes of mercy toward us, and after this our exile, show unto us the blessed fruit of thy womb, Jesus. O clement, O loving, O sweet Virgin Mary!

Leader: Pray for us, O Holy Mother of God,

All: That we may be worthy of the promises of Christ. *(Optional)*

Leader: Let us pray.

All: Oh God, whose only begotten Son by his life, death, and resurrection has purchased for us the rewards of eternal life; grant, we beseech thee, that meditating on these mysteries of the Most Holy Rosary of the Blessed Virgin Mary, we may imitate what they contain and obtain what they promise, through the same Christ our Lord. Amen.

Introductory Prayers

You start the Rosary by holding the crucifix while making a Sign of the Cross and then reciting the Apostles' Creed.

Then, holding the short stem which holds the cross on the set of Rosary beads:

- Recite the "Our Father" on the first large bead.
- Say a "Hail Mary" for an increase of faith, hope and charity on each of the three small beads.
- Recite the "Glory Be to the Father" on the large bead.
- Recite the Fatima Prayer on the same large bead.
- Recall the first Rosary Mystery and recite the "Our Father" on the same large bead.

The Main Part of the Rosary

- On each of the following ten small beads (also called a decade) say a "Hail Mary" while reflecting on the mystery.
- On the next large bead, recite the "Glory Be to the Father" and the Fatima prayer.
- Each succeeding decade is prayed in a similar

manner by recalling the appropriate mystery, reciting the "Our Father", ten "Hail Marys", the "Glory Be to the Father", and the Fatima prayer while reflecting on the mystery.

- When the fifth mystery is completed, the Rosary is then concluded with the "Hail Holy Queen" and the Sign of the Cross.

Signs of What's Ahead

19

Armageddon

The time is very near. I believe that this generation will witness the Second Coming of Christ on Earth. We are now being asked by God through his messenger Our Blessed Mother to prepare ourselves for the arrival of Jesus the Christ on this Earth. The messages given to me by Our Lady at Knock are significant in their timing.

Jesus is coming back to Earth to conquer the Antichrist and his armies and to gather together and restore the nation of Israel. His Second Coming will be at the end of the Tribulation, the seven years of turmoil in the world, and at the time of the war of Armageddon. And this will happen soon.

The good news is that his Coming will herald a new beginning. A new glorious era of tremendous peace, love and happiness on Earth. But, unfortunately, this won't happen until after we experience a huge and horrible turmoil on this Earth brought about by the

Antichrist. Even the believers will suffer – but at the hands of Satan. We could well now be at the start of the Tribulation period. World financial markets have already collapsed, earthquakes and world disasters are increasing in intensity and people's faith in God has rapidly disappeared. In its place grows the new "cool" rational thinking that is atheism.

Many Christians believe, rightly, that God is merciful and that therefore he would not allow his followers to suffer, but the reality is that God's ways are not ours. The good and the bad will suffer during this time. It is an inescapable fact. We will all witness what's ahead before we are saved. But prayer and strong faith will be powerful weapons in the fight against the Antichrist.

Remember, even God's most faithful followers will suffer for their belief. Christians, since the beginning of time, have always suffered for their faith. This time their faith will be put to an even greater test.

So, are the Signs here Already?

The Antichrist is here now. He who is without a soul is already scheming and planning to win over souls. All with the help of an army of powerful world influencers. As I write the final chapters in this book he is preparing to wage war on the human race in ways that are unimaginable. While he is doing this so, too, will the wrath of God's will descend on the world to warn us of the changes that are about to happen.

The truth is I do not know the time, the date or the place of the Second Coming. No one does. No one will in advance. For that is made very clear in the Bible. But one thing I do know from the clear messages I am receiving from Our Lady, and that is the time is getting very close now and it could be within the next five to ten years.

I take no pleasure in revealing this information. The pain I have gone through when I have been shown the visions of what lies ahead on our planet has been excruciating. I know that other visionaries are being shown the same visions right now in the world and secrets are also being revealed to them.

Our Lady has urged me to reveal the truth so that souls can be saved before it is too late. I hope that my revelations will encourage everyone to consider opening up their hearts to God again. To accept the truth, all of which is contained in her "Father's Holy Book". People must allow God to come back into their lives again. We need to save ourselves and be prepared to stand up and be prepared to acknowledge his existence.

By praying, not only will they save themselves but they will save their entire family from the snares of the Deceiver – the Evil One. Not only that, but through powerful prayer and through groups who pray together, some disasters can be averted through the mercy of the Good Lord. But not all. Because all of what is about to happen has been prophesied. Armageddon will happen. The final battle between God and the Antichrist will take place. Be reassured though that the Antichrist will be beaten. Sadly some people will mistakenly follow the Antichrist, believing in his false teachings. They will be the ultimate losers.

The Signs to Watch Out For

God has given us some of the signs and warnings to prepare us for what's ahead. To give us another chance to seek redemption. Many of us have failed to notice these signs for what they are. And while God is ever loving and forgiving, make no mistake He will stamp out the evil in the world. Even if that means true followers will suffer. The wrath of God is very real and something we should be aware of. We can expect to see more world catastrophes as His time to return to Earth gets closer.

The earthquakes, tsunamis and frequent flooding are just some examples in which the Hand of God works. These disasters are not accidental. They will continue to get worse until the Second Coming. Meanwhile the Antichrist, as prophesied in the Book of Revelation is getting prepared. And he is exceptionally organised and is getting the results he wants. People have lost their faith in God around the world. It's reaching epidemic proportions as atheism grows. These people are beyond hope and I pray for them every day.

I believe that the following events will unfold just as prophesied. I believe we will see the collapse and destruction of large international cities – sophisticated modern cities – which will come about as the Wrath of God descends.

A new form of evil control in the world is now underway. The evidence will be seen shortly. This is the most sinister and devastating disaster of all because it is so highly deceptive. It is so deceptive that people like me will be ridiculed for suggesting that it exists. I will be deemed a head-case, a fanatic and someone with an overactive imagination. But let me assure you that this is already happening. It will be achieved through the power of control. Real control. If you want to control people what three areas do you target? Money of course. Politics would come a close second. Followed by Religion.

Managed behind secret organisations with powerful strands in every country in the world, the core power lies in a tightly knit network of powerful people in the top tiers of the organisations. They meet regularly, have global secret conferences, hold special "satanic" ceremonies behind closed doors. And they obey his instructions very carefully. We will, despite our efforts to fight it, come totally under the control of this global network which will cover Church,

Politics and Banking (the three key areas which exert control over all our lives).

It is comprised of a highly controlled, methodical and secretive team of very powerful leaders – all of whom are working with the Antichrist. And it's being done in absolute secrecy. So cunning are they that even those within the organisations at the lower levels haven't a clue what's going on.

The Result? I believe we will see one major banking organisation come into being, disguised behind democracy and portrayed as being a very "reasonable and sound" solution to the international banking crisis. It will be launched and presented as being great news for everyone – no more bank crashes. At last we will have a bank that cannot, just cannot fail! And we will buy into this idea. But it will become apparent very quickly that we have lost control. Not only of our personal finances but our ability to buy food, shelter, medicine and healthcare. Our hands will be tied. Cash will be a thing of the past. Each one of us will have to use a card. More than likely it will have a chip. Everyone will be accounted for and our rights to data protection will vanish. Be assured that the number of the Beast, 666, will be contained within this card. The Bible states that it will be stamped on everyone. In the modern world it will more than likely appear on something that we take for granted and won't question. And more than likely something not visible to the naked eye.

In politics we will see a leader emerge who will work closely with the other two powerful figures – the one in banking and the leader of a new Church. They will be seen as the "dream team" and will be admired by many.

A new Church will emerge. It will be heralded as being for the good of all. It will not be a Christian Church but will be portrayed as such. This Church itself will be run by the most charismatic leader – charming, intelligent, influential and evil. For he will be the Antichrist – and just one of a team of three. And people will believe he is the real Christ.

"*Take heed that ye be not deceived: for many shall come in my name, saying, I am Christ; and the time draweth near: go ye not therefore after them.*" (Luke 21:8)

So when the Antichrist stands in the "Temple of God" – launches a new Church – people will mistakenly believe him to be the real God. This event is close. As the Catholic Church continues to be tormented this Antichrist will, in my view, either take up position and replace the Pope or he will launch a completely different Church. Who knows? But it will happen. So now is the time for Christians to prepare to fight.

And just as it clearly states in the Bible that as Jesus ascended into Heaven when leaving this Earth he declared that he would come back to judge the living and the dead, I believe he will come back.

Acts 1:9–11

"And as they were gazing intently into the sky while He was departing, behold, two men in white clothing stood beside them; and they also said, "Men of Galilee, why do you stand looking up into the sky? This Jesus, who has been taken up from you into Heaven, will come in just the same way as you have watched Him go into Heaven."

Before that time I believe he will give us a number of warnings – warnings that will be difficult for us not to notice. The believers will fall to their knees in love and awe while the sceptics will either be converted or simply turn their back and refuse to acknowledge the truth.

"What must I do to be saved?" The answer was, *"Believe in the Lord Jesus Christ, and thou shalt be saved"* (Acts 16:30–31).

THE END

Appendix

The Witnesses

Here are some samples of the many witness accounts.

Paddy Smith, County Mayo

On the 11th of October 2010, I went to Knock with my wife to see for myself what all the hype about the apparition was for. I had heard on the radio of Joe Coleman's prediction of the apparition due to take place in Knock on that date. So we arrived early that day and we were lucky to find a seat in the Apparition Chapel. Very soon afterwards, the chapel filled to capacity. People were then squeezing in the doorway, trying to get a glimpse of what was happening inside. Thousands were outside.

We were kneeling down and everyone was saying the Rosary shortly before 3 p.m. when Joe Coleman and the late Keith Henderson, the visionaries, walked to the front of the altar with a large wooden cross held in front of them. Keith went up before the statue of Our Lady and started to pray. Then he was joined by Joe Coleman. They were both in a trance and seemed to be communicating with Our Lady. To me, having been in Medjugorje, they behaved the very same way as the visionaries there when they went into the trance. They never moved a muscle and kept absolutely still while looking up. Keith was smiling the whole time but Joe was crying.

Then, on coming back to their seats, Joe turned to everyone and told us all that Our Lady had said to him to tell us to "watch the sun". People then turned around to look outside the window. We could see the sun peeping out from behind the clouds, which were dark. And then a black cloud moved away quickly and the sun came right out of the sky. It began to get bigger and bigger, as if it was coming down towards the people. Many people were getting distressed and frightened at what they were witnessing.

Then, the sun went back into position again but, fairly quickly, it started to change colours. First a mixture of red and blue until a white host shape covered it up, which seemed to be pulsating and overlapping the sun. We were astonished and couldn't believe what we were seeing.

Still sitting in our seats in the chapel, we looked up again to see that the sun had changed to the most beautiful shade of green. It stayed green for some time. Some people were still crying and distressed and overcome with emotion.

I then saw a black cross in the sky, right under the sun. I looked again just to make sure. Yes, it definitely was a tall black elegant cross – as clear as anything. I looked around, then back up towards the altar at Our Lady's statue, because I had heard people say, "Look at the statue." To my amazement, it was covered by a golden mist. Some of the golden mist was even visible on the wall. It stayed like this for some time, just as the sun did. I'd say in total the whole series of events lasted half an hour.

On 31st October 2009 we went to Knock again for the next predicted apparition. This time we were in the larger church, usually used to accommodate the large pilgrimages – the Basilica Church. I was shocked to see the church crammed with so many people, thousands in fact. Many people had to be turned away and the church doors shut because it couldn't fit any more people. The rest stayed outside and they nearly filled the whole area outside, as so many people showed up.

Joe and Keith, the visionaries, were at the altar. They were surrounded by lots of press photographers, all crowded in around them but cordoned off, so we could see them clearly. They went into a trance just towards the end of the Rosary and I could see the tears flowing down Joe's face. Keith, though, was in a similar trance but was smiling the entire time.

Then, immediately the Rosary was finished, a great rumbling sound could be heard from the roof – like thunder – then a bang. We didn't know what it was, but it was definitely coming from the roof, as if it was a flash of lightning. With that, people began shouting from outside and many people rushed out. Hundreds and hundreds of people dashed outside the church. We could hear them from where we were sitting, shouting to each other, "Look at the sun, look at the sun."

We decided to go outside then. Just as we got to the door, though, we met a woman we know from the area who was very, very excited. She told us that she had just seen a vision of Our Lady, clearly visible on the wall behind the altar, holding the Baby Jesus in her arms. It happened, she said, just as the Rosary was finishing. She was still overcome. I know this woman and she is a very sound person and of sound mind, so I believed her.

As we made our way outside the church, through the throngs of people, we could hear so many people crying and praying out loud. We looked up and couldn't believe our eyes. The sun was – how can I put it? – just dancing in the sky! It looked different to the last time. Now it dazzled and sparkled and, because there was no glare, you could look at it very easily. It was such a spectacle. It kept dancing and changing colour so many times. Then it would spin across the sky. It lasted such a long time, for at least half an hour. We were overcome with emotion.

One woman close to us, from our local town, revealed that earlier on the sun had turned green and formed into what looked to her like a map of Ireland. Again this woman is someone we have known for many years. She is practical, down to Earth and of very high standing, so we believed her. We had no reason to doubt her. Something very special was happening and we were so privileged to have witnessed these events.

Denise Long from Galway,
mother of three teenage children

I first read about the apparitions in the paper and followed the story. My son came to me on the 12th of October 2009 and told me that his friend had been down in Knock the day before, on the 11th of October. When he told me that his friend had witnessed the sun dance in the sky and change colour, I paid very little attention. I was also annoyed. I said to my son, "This guy is making a right idiot of you! Don't be so ridiculous. How can the sun change and dance in the sky?"

However, coming up to the time of the apparition on the 31st of October, my curiosity got the better of me. I persuaded my husband to travel to Knock just to see what all the hype was about. We arrived at 1.30 p.m., thinking that we would be nice and early. To our astonishment, the Basilica was almost full at that stage. Despite the fact that we hadn't really eaten earlier and this was the last chance my husband had to grab a bite to eat, I wouldn't let him. And so in we went and got seats for my husband, my daughter and myself.

While we waited for the Rosary to begin, I happened to speak with an elderly lady sitting next to me. She explained that she had been there on the 11th of October and had witnessed the sun dance in the sky. She was still in shock over what she had seen.

Then the event began and turned into what I can only describe as an utter shambles. Because the Knock officials refused to put a microphone on the altar, it meant that we couldn't hear people trying to say the Rosary. While some people attempted to shout it out as loud as they could on one side, people on the other side of the church were trying to pick up what was being said. Apart from there being no microphone on the altar, there were no flowers. The place was dismal, bare and empty. Unbelievable. To think that Knock knew that thousands of people would show up and hadn't the courtesy to allow sound in the church was insulting to those attending on the day.

As I looked around at the masses of people jammed everywhere, I noticed that there were only about four security people in the church. It was hard to believe when you looked at the crowds.

Eventually the Rosary commenced and everyone joined in. Then, when the Rosary had just finished, I heard a loud bang coming from the roof, as if something had hit it. Shortly after that, we heard people shouting from outside and then people began to race out of the church. People in front of us were coming towards us. We were afraid we would be trampled on, so we began to run as well outside the church. We were no sooner outside than we looked up to see what everyone was talking about.

A cloud had parted and this luminous sun appeared. It was a vibrant reddish gold colour and began to bounce up and down! Then it changed to a vibrant yellow and everything around us seemed to go yellow all of a sudden, and not a reflection of the sun. Everyone was looking at each other saying, "Look, you are yellow!" Then it changed to purple. Then to a pure white with a hint of a black ring around it. Looking up again, I was dumbstruck when I saw a single cross in black against the white background of the sun. I thought, *Has the world ended? Have I died? This couldn't happen to me on Earth!* I knew that something extraordinary and mysterious – not of this world – was happening. I looked around then desperately, in a daze, for an explanation of sorts – from anyone – my husband, my daughter, a stranger. But they were trying to deal with this phenomenon themselves.

A lot of people had fallen on their knees and I could hear them reciting the Hail Mary and shouting out to Our Lady. People, strangers, were hugging each other. People were crying. Some were confessing their sins out loud, for everyone to hear. But no one was listening to them. We were too overcome with pure love. We all became one that day. A strange thing to say, but strangers, that day, acted like they were one big happy family.

Overjoyed, I almost felt guilty that I was given such a rare gift and was so privileged to see such a miracle with my own eyes, something no one expects to see in this life. I immediately rang my mother on my mobile.

"Mam, you won't believe . . . won't believe what I've just witnessed . . ." Then I rambled on.

"Denise, you're are not making sense," she said. "What's going on?"

I told her about the sun dancing. "The sun? I don't believe it. You've got to be kidding. Did you really see it? Are you sure you didn't imagine it?" And then she believed me because she knows me. She was "over the moon".

Less than ten minutes later, my sister rang me from Chicago, because my mother had phoned her to tell her what was happening. She was ecstatic and crying on the phone. She is now coming with her boyfriend and his parents from Chicago to Ireland to attend the next apparition predicted by Joe Coleman.

I heard a lot of other stories about events that took place that day. People had been told that water began to pour from the healing rock – an old stone from the outer wall of the original chapel at Knock. It has been known to water before, but that day it oozed.

Then there was the case of the sun's reflection in the Apparition Chapel, where one wall is made completely of glass and was in the eye of the sun at that time. One man had heard from people that the sun was not reflecting off the glass. I spoke with this man and he explained that he walked over to the window to investigate. A normal sun would reflect into a window. When he looked into the window of the apparition chapel, there was no reflection or evidence of any sun. Yet it was beaming down on top of everyone.

Going home exhausted, I couldn't help reminding myself that I had come down to see what all this rubbish was about. And now I was converted for life. The sad thing was, though, I was very careful whom I told. After all, people will think you're mad when you tell them what happened. I know I met so many people that day who saw what I saw. I saw the thousands looking up, awestruck, at the sun dancing in the sky. Yet very few would come forward for fear of ridicule.

I witnessed the sun dancing again on the 22nd of February 2010 in Knock, which Joe Coleman had predicted. And it was beautiful. It lasted an amazing fifty minutes but it was not as strong as the one on the 31st of October. Nevertheless, it danced and dazzled again, just as predicted.

Then on the 10th of March, we saw the sun dance again immediately after the apparition. I was shocked and very hurt to see, though, the way we were treated at the Knock Shrine. During the Rosary that day, a man who works in the Knock Shrine office looked in the window at the side of the church while we were saying the Rosary. To my disgust, he nodded his head from side to side in the most condescending way imaginable – laughing at us.

The Rosary was then interrupted by a priest who began to say Mass, even though no Mass had been planned for that chapel. I know because I phoned the Shrine afterwards. I was told in no uncertain terms that Mass is not said in the chapel, it is held in the other one. It would be a very rare occasion, if at all, that Mass would be said there.

I was so upset afterwards, as were other people that day. These people tried to "put us off" and did everything they could to interrupt the Rosary and our devotion to Our Lady. How dare they? They ought to be ashamed of themselves, especially as they, supposedly, represent one of the most holy shrines in Europe. We cannot deny what we saw and owe Our Lady that. We owe it to her. All we can think of now, morning, noon and night, is what we witnessed.

Has it changed my life? As a Catholic I always had a belief and I did go to Mass. Now, though, my faith has become very strong. I tend to be more aware of God, more conscious of practising the faith. Our family now goes to confession more often. We pray more and all the family, including the children, pray together. Also, a neighbour of ours comes down to us every single night to say the Rosary.

Danielle Walsh from Dublin

The first time I went to Knock I saw the sun dance in the sky and where the moon and the sun seemed to come together and merge, with a black ring around them. Then the sun began to spin. I couldn't believe what I was seeing at first. But as I stood there I knew that it was not natural – it wasn't something that you could explain. The more it began to sparkle and spin, the more dumbstruck I became. I was puzzled, unsure what I was looking at. What could it be? Was it a sign of some sort? I found it all so difficult to take in. For days, weeks afterwards, I couldn't get it out of my mind. But I still wasn't sure what exactly I had seen and what it meant.

I decided I would have to go again to Knock on the 22nd of February. I hadn't been at the other apparitions since the first one on the 11th of October. There were about sixty people in the church as myself and my sister Louise arrived. I felt really warm in the church just as the Rosary was being said. Then, near the end of the Rosary, I looked at the statue of Our Lady and saw a mist form around the base of the statue. Then I saw her in the full flesh float from the statue. Shocked, I couldn't move. My heart was thumping. I felt dizzy. I couldn't see her face clearly, but I saw white and gold stars lighting around her whole body.

Then, as we continued to say the Rosary I looked and couldn't believe it – she was moving her lips and she seemed to be saying the Rosary with us!

Then a strange thing happened. Her face changed

into Our Lord's – I could see a vision of Him, dazzling in a mist of white and gold. I noticed that he had a short dark beard. Then everyone in the church seemed to disappear. I was on my own facing the vision with what seemed to be like many torches flickering – I couldn't see anyone else in the church. My heart filled up then. This incredible presence touched my heart and my whole body. I was touched with love and peace like I have never felt before in my life. Then, as soon as it was over, I was back in the church, the Rosary was finished and I could see Joe Coleman kneeling in the front seat of the church, right in front of the altar, in a complete trance.

After that experience, I felt that I had no choice but to go back. How could I not?

On the 10th of March 2010, during the last part of the Rosary, which was being said out loud by everyone in the Apparition Chapel, I felt dizziness sweep over me and began to feel an incredible heat.

Our Lady this time formed from out of the statue. She floated in a maze of white and gold dazzling lights around her. This time I could see her more clearly than before and noticed the details. She was wearing a white gown and blue dress. I could see her face was pale but one thing I couldn't ignore because it was so strong: it was the pure love in her eyes. Immediately I burst into tears. My body started shaking from head to toe. I looked down for a second or two and then, as I raised my eyes to look at her again, I couldn't believe it when I saw that she was now holding the Baby Jesus in her arms. Her eyes were cast down and she looked sad. I could feel the woman beside me shaking and crying, so I supposed she was seeing Our Lady as well. I couldn't stop crying at that stage.

I then became aware that we were now in the middle of a Mass. I hadn't noticed the priest coming out onto the altar during all of this.

But I couldn't resist looking back at Our Lady. To my astonishment, her face changed, as before, into Our Lord's face. At that point I had to stop. I had to look away. It was so overwhelming, I couldn't take it all in. Then I pulled myself together and I said to Our Lady, "It's okay if you want to come again." But she had gone at that stage. I was so sad afterwards. Even though I was overjoyed and full of love, I was sad because she was so sad.

Since all of this has happened, my life will never be the same again. I have found faith. I also feel now a certain peace and calmness that I never had before. I think about it a lot, about the good side of life. Life has taken on much more meaning. I know now for sure that God really does exist.

Pat O'Toole

I was cured of kidney cancer after I visited Knock on 31st October 2009. I had heard the reports of what had happened on 11th October, so I decided to see what was happening.

Suffering from cancer of the right kidney and awaiting surgery to have the kidney removed, I felt that anything was worth trying to look for a cure. During the Rosary I felt a great sense of peace in me that I can't explain and felt tearful. After the Rosary was said in the church, I heard a loud bang from the roof and then a commotion when people began to charge out of the church. I followed the crowds outside, only to see the most incredible sight you can imagine. As I looked up at the sun, it began to spin and seemed to be shaking from side to side. It turned a beautiful golden colour and it was very easy to look at it, because it seemed to have a circular host covering it. I can't explain but it did things that a normal sun doesn't do! Spinning, dancing, changing colour, it went on for over half an hour. At one point I noticed that everyone around us seemed to have a golden glow around them. Everything seemed to turn a yellowish gold; it touched everyone.

The following day I suffered excruciating pain. Bedridden, I could hardly breathe with the pain. I was in total agony. The day after that, I went to the doctor and told him about the pain the previous day and explained that I was no longer in pain. I asked him what it meant – had the cancer spread?

As the time for my operation drew close, they gave me a scan in the hospital. To the surprise and shock of my doctors, no trace of cancer could be detected. None whatsoever. I felt fine and healthy, and I haven't looked back. It was a miracle cure, without question.

~

Since the apparitions, there have been a reported seven people who claim to have seen visions of Our Lady in the church and who, at the time of writing this book, have all plucked up the courage to come forward. Four cures have been reported, including one woman who had lost the sight in her left eye completely for many years and found she could see again after the apparition on October 31st. Another woman with severe arthritis in her leg found that it had completely disappeared during the episode of the sun dancing on October 31st.

For the many thousands who were present at the apparitions, the experience has completely converted them to a profound belief. For others who have heard from family and friends of their experiences, it has helped them find their faith again.